Beyond Tribal Lines

Reimagining Communities and Boundaries in Africa

Adam B. Seligman

Charles Esibikhwa Edward

First Edition: February 2025

Published by: Nsemia Inc. (www.nsemia.com)

Editor: Nsemia Inc.

Cover Concept: Authors

Cover Illustration: Robert Kambo

Cover Design: Linda Kiboma

Layout Design: Bethsheba Nyabuto

Note for Librarians:

A cataloguing record for this book is available from Kenya National Library Services

ISBN: 978-9914-760-27-9

Acknowledgement

"We would like to thank the many Communities Engaging with Difference and Religion (CEDAR) teams in East Africa, Asia, the Middle East, and Europe without whose dedication and commitment these past 25 years, this book would not have come into existence."

What Others Say

"This book should be a must-read by the policymakers and all communities."

- George Oyeho, PhD, Tangaza University College.

"Firstly, I'll begin by thanking the authors for gifting Africa, and I dare say, the world a wholesome guideline to cohabiting despite differences. Going through the 11 rules, I couldn't help but get emotional thinking, 'Finally, we've hacked tribalism!'. This book is recommended to every political, academic, religious, and societal leader, especially the aspirers. The breadth of case studies from West, Central, East, and South Africa shows how similar and common these tribal realities prevail in different political boundaries."

- David Owumi, Founder, Executive Director, Salt House—Institute for Inclusive Governance and Sustainable Development, Lagos, Nigeria.

"This challenging book is valuable on multiple levels. For peacebuilders and people of goodwill, it provides fresh awareness and helpful hints as a potential playbook for facilitating effective community building among diverse populations. Though focused on the African experience, Beyond Tribal Lines also offers insights that are applicable elsewhere in a world that is increasingly vulnerable to polarization and fear of the other."

- Terry D. Bergdall, PhD, The Asset Based Community Development (ABCD) Institute, DePaul University, author of Methods for Active Participation: Experiences in Rural Development from East and Central Africa.

"Beyond Tribal Lines: Reimagining Communities and Boundaries in Africa is a rare book, one filled not only with insight but also intended to be read collectively. Reading is often a solitary activity, yet by design, the authors have created a work that not only discusses the importance of community but also engages readers in ways that facilitate the renewal or creation of communities. The language is thought-provoking yet accessible, intended to expand readers' understandings of boundaries and community, belonging and difference, and doing so in a way that allows readers to make the text personal by relating their own experiences throughout the text."

- *David W. Montgomery, Research Professor, Department of Government and Politics and the Center for International Development and Conflict Management, University of Maryland, USA.*

Table Contents

Prologue and Problem

Whatever other events may emerge to characterize the 21st century, one phenomenon is by now pretty well established: the challenge of living with difference is coming to define political, social, and cultural realities throughout the world. By "living with difference" we mean living with, accommodating, and sharing a public life—in city streets, schools, shops, hospitals, yoga studios, sports clubs, youth groups and so on—with people whose religious beliefs, political commitments and convictions, ways of life, foods, sexual preferences, dress, habits, family arrangements, skin colour, mother tongues, physiognomies and cultural loyalties may be different from our own. In brief, it means sharing a civic life with people emerging from, and living in, different communities.

Historically, this reality of diversity is not new to Africa. The continent is home to thousands of ethnic groups, cultures, and languages, all coexisting within the borders of modern states. Kingdoms and empires like Mali, Great Zimbabwe, Buganda, the Kingdom of Aksum, the Songhai Empire, the Kingdom of Kongo, the Benin Kingdom, the Ashanti Empire, the Kingdom of Mapungubwe, and the Oyo Empire were all marked by ethnic diversity and cultural plurality. Yet, the creation of modern African nation-states by colonial powers introduced an ideal of political and ethnic homogeneity that has often resulted in tensions and conflicts, particularly when states were drawn along artificial borders.

In fact, and throughout the world, the emergence of the modern nation-state was accompanied to a greater or lesser extent by attempts to homogenize the population so that all citizens would share one language, one cuisine, one idea of home and belonging, and one moral vision and definition of community. In Africa, this was often reinforced through state policies that prioritized certain ethnic groups or languages, such as Kiswahili in Tanzania or Amharic in Ethiopia. This push for national unity and uniformity mirrored the nation-building efforts seen elsewhere, and just as in other parts of the world, it often led to the marginalization of minority groups and the suppression of diverse cultural expressions.

The roots of many of these African challenges can be traced back to the Treaty of Berlin (also known as the Berlin Conference of 1884–1885, where European colonial powers arbitrarily divided Africa into territories without regard to the existing ethnic, linguistic, or cultural boundaries. This event laid the foundation for the modern African nation-states, which were often composed of multiple, distinct communities forced to coexist within artificially drawn borders. The Berlin Conference effectively set the stage for future conflicts, as diverse groups were expected to form national identities under the imposed structures of governance. The colonial legacy of dividing and ruling communities further complicated post-colonial efforts to build cohesive, unified nation-states, leading to long-term ethnic tensions and conflicts that continue to resonate in various parts of the continent today.

The combination of colonial boundaries and post-colonial policies of homogenization has created an enduring struggle for many African countries, as they grapple with the need to forge national unity while respecting the rich diversity of their populations.

Moreover, and critically, this ideal of national homogeneity in Africa was often defined in terms of ethnic dominance, where one group sought to assert its identity, culture, and language over others. This conceit can be traced back to pre-colonial rivalries and was exacerbated by colonial policies that favoured certain ethnic groups over others, such as the British support of the Tutsi in Rwanda and Burundi or the promotion of the Shona over the Ndebele in Zimbabwe. The legacy of ethnic favouritism has persisted post-independence, with ruling elites in many countries promoting their ethnic group as the national identity, marginalizing others. This drive for ethnic dominance continues to fascinate and divide, leading to violence and conflict, as seen in the Rwandan Genocide of 1994 or the civil wars in South Sudan and Ethiopia, even in recent times.

Despite the nostalgic sentiments many hold towards an imagined past of ethnic or cultural purity and uniformity, Africa's current social reality increasingly resists such conformity. Various factors contribute to this shift. In Africa, demographic changes, the impact of climate change, and ecological crises, such as droughts and desertification, have driven large-scale internal displacement and migration. Conflicts such as the insurgency in northern

Mozambique or the displacement from the Sahel region have led to a rise in refugees and migrants moving across the continent. Furthermore, the rise of "identity politics," where ethnic and regional groups seek recognition and representation in political and social spaces, has deepened divides.

The post-colonial state in Africa faces political fracturing, often exacerbated by ethnic tensions, as seen most recently in countries like Ethiopia and South Sudan. The increasing use of social media has added fuel to these tensions, eroding the shared public sphere and enabling divisive narratives to spread. These changes demand that African societies learn to navigate differences in a world far more complex than the one that emerged post-independence. Learning to live with difference, amidst deep-rooted identities, is one of the continent's most pressing challenges.

The long-term consequences of policies and events like the mass movement of labourers across colonial territories in Africa, the forced displacement during the apartheid era in South Africa, and the resettlement of populations after decolonization, are just some examples of much wider shifts in African societies. For instance, the recruitment of migrant workers from rural to urban areas under colonial rule, the movement of ethnic groups across borders drawn arbitrarily by colonial powers, and post-colonial internal migration in search of economic opportunities have significantly transformed the dynamics of sameness and difference within African nation-states. These developments have realigned the nature of boundaries between ethnic and regional communities, often exacerbating existing tensions or giving rise to new ones as people struggle to redefine belonging in rapidly changing social landscapes.

The sum of these developments and consequent changes in the social configuration of national states has resulted in the need to confront difference in a manner few have been accustomed to and this, as we are coming to see, is evolving as no small challenge. While these challenges have most often been discussed in terms of policy orientations or of the political philosophy of liberalism, we claim that facing the continual challenges of difference demands of us a reassessment of our attitudes toward community, toward its boundaries, and, in fact, to our own sense of self. We argue that to approach this social reality of radical difference, in a civil as well as ethical manner, demands of us nothing less than a willingness to be uncomfortable and to eschew the deceptive comforts that certain contemporary approaches to communities and their boundaries tend to promulgate. Facing difference with eyes wide open is a serious challenge that requires us to tolerate or bear a degree and type of discomfort to which we are unaccustomed. But such practices can be learned, as so much of the social world is.

Living with difference is uncomfortable. It challenges our sense of belonging and identity. But it is also necessary, especially in a rapidly changing Africa. The discomfort of facing differences head-on is part of the work of building inclusive, peaceful societies. This book argues that as we encounter unprecedented levels of diversity, we must learn to bear this discomfort and develop new ways of engaging with difference. Through these principles of social re-engagement, we can begin to navigate the complexities of belonging in Africa today preserving the integrity of our communities while opening up to others. The rules presented here are a minimum guide to reclaiming that shared sense of belonging in an increasingly diverse world.

In a world where identities intersect and diverge in infinite ways—be it ethnicity, clan, class, or subclan—appreciating the value of living with difference is not just a lofty ideal but a practical necessity. Caring about difference has profound both for individuals and for humanity as a whole.

At an individual level, embracing difference enriches our lives. Engaging with those who think, live, and believe differently from us expands our perspectives and deepens our understanding of the world. It challenges us to step out of the narrow confines of our personal experiences and see life through another's eyes. This not only makes us more empathetic and adaptable but also fosters personal growth, as we learn to navigate complexities with humility and grace. In a society where diverse ideas, skills, and knowledge interact, individuals stand to gain better opportunities for collaboration, innovation, and self-discovery.

On a collective level, living with difference is foundational to building peaceful and thriving communities. The divisions that arise from ethnic, clan, and class differences often lead to conflict, distrust, and stagnation. However, when communities choose to embrace their diversity, they unlock the potential for resilience, creativity, and unity. Just as ecosystems thrive on biodiversity, human societies flourish when they harness the strengths of their differences rather than suppressing them. Appreciating these distinctions allows us to work together to address shared challenges, from climate change to economic inequality, in ways that no homogenous group could achieve alone.

But beyond these practical gains, there is a moral imperative to living with difference. Humanity's survival has always depended on our ability to cooperate and coexist despite our divisions. In an age of growing polarization, this principle becomes ever more urgent. Living with difference affirms our shared humanity; it is a recognition that, despite our varied histories, cultures, and circumstances, we are all interconnected. The act of reaching across divides—whether of tribe, wealth, or status—becomes an expression of hope, a belief that we can transcend the barriers that separate us and create a world where everyone belongs.

Ultimately, the question is "what kind of future do we want?" By choosing to live with difference, we make a deliberate commitment to a future where diversity is not a source of conflict but a wellspring of possibility. Whether we are commoners or royalty, members of the same ethnic group or different ones, our ability to thrive depends on our willingness to coexist, collaborate, and build a shared vision of a better world.

In sum, the logic of this short book is that communities carry their own requirements of membership, implicit and explicit. In the face of growing encounters of deep difference at a scale not seen before—and the likelihood of global migration to increase—there is a need for guiding principles, or rules, for developing the skills to live with others who are different. This does not mean trivializing the importance of boundaries or community. Rather, we present the minimum of what must be kept in mind as we reclaim the thickness of belonging in the world today.

Foreword

This short text is a profound meditation on the often unacknowledged feelings about the other and the other community. It is a primer and a treatise at the same time, as well as a clear, well-structured and informative text about perceptions, understandings and experiences of community, of boundaries and of difference. It is also a learning tool and a resource for conflict prevention and conflict resolution for learners and facilitators on programmes strengthening social cohesion. The central theme throughout is difference, the nature of social difference, difference in its many manifestations, difference in its many lived experiences, and community difference at local and national levels; and it is about the solutions learners find themselves on how to share public spaces – our markets, our streets, our schools, our hospitals. It's a book on dealing with difference.

At the end of the book, the reader realizes how much ground has been covered in such a short space. And yet, the text is not crowded. Short bursts of intensity are quickly relieved by turning to imagined lived experiences and imagined anecdotes, those previous scenarios. One of the gems of the book is to leave to our imagination the narratives or memories that workshop participants recount, those previous scenarios re-imagined that they retell in order to make abstract notions real to them.

Somehow, Seligman and Esibikhwa have drawn on their shared and individual knowledge of many countries and communities spanning several continents, without allowing international experience to weigh down or slow down the thrust of the book.

The context of difference is explained. In Africa, and elsewhere, recent migrations have led to new and unprecedented mingling of communities, in-country migrations and cross-border migrations, individual and group migrations, and systemic and *ad hoc* migrations. It could be said that population movement is an exciting phenomenon, bringing peoples closer together. It could be. However, local and global experience shows that the results are mixed. We join the authors in declaring an urgency for giving hosts and migrants the opportunity to learn new skills for living with diversity. Learners are the target audience of this book. They are people around the world who want to make change, the soon-to-be facilitators, community members, social policy and programme shapers, and the public at large.

Pertinent to the theme of difference in Africa is the historic drive to unify and homogenize the arbitrarily created colonial territories, initiated at the Berlin Conference in 1884-1885. The trend continues. In the post-independence decade of the 1960s, African governments enthusiastically espoused national policies of unification and homogenization, with the laudable intention of welding nationhood. However, at the same time, the fracturing of some of those same nation-states and the marginalization of some communities within them are a constant threat and carry the seeds of cultural and social exclusion of some communities while interrogating the core of the state.

The title of the book may shock at first, or the word 'tribal'. There is no hiding behind the term 'ethnic'. Unflinching, the authors signal from the start where the problem lies. They trace the journey of their programme learners. Throughout the book, and in an increasingly positive vein, many options for action are revealed to the reader, through the learning experience of the learners themselves, as readers imagine them grappling with the questions and role play at the end of each chapter. The concepts of boundaries and difference in this manageable book are probed. Participants come eventually to relate these initially theoretical concepts to their own lives. The notion of *community* comes to prevail - and in so many positive dimensions.

Communities are defined by their boundaries. But boundaries differ greatly in type, spanning boundaries of land, of property, of ethnicity, of jurisdiction, of generations, of gender, of religion, of urban or rural identity, bodily boundaries, and more. These are communities with varying degrees of fastness of borders. Some are well-recognized conceptual or physical borders with distinct membership while others have more tenuous boundaries. Seligman and Esibikhwa go out of their way to get readers to imagine even more types of boundaries defining groups or communities.

They point out that boundaries are also spaces for inter-communal interaction. And boundaries are fluid over time. The authors envisage the development of neighbourhoods where difference is not only tolerated but where neighbours actively accept, negotiate, and navigate their way through their city or their village.

The book weaves through many themes but ever present is the constant application of knowledge and experience to learning new behavioural skills. Those themes include the familiar and the unfamiliar, curiosity about the other, discomfort in their presence, or tension, a feeling of risk, of threat of danger and experienced danger; feelings of shame or guilt; tense situations experiences and may be shared in the presence of other sacred traditions, concepts of compromise, experience of the non-negotiable becoming amenable to accommodation. The new behavioural skills acquired include listening skills, keener observation, and more thoughtful and efficient negotiating tactics, all gleaned from practice with the new skills on remembered, lived experience – going back and acting differently, going forward and still practising. Those skills are intended to be honed by sustained practice in real life.

Anna P. Obura PhD

Teacher, education planner, peace education developer, and practitioner on many fronts; former Education Advisor, UNICEF, Eastern and Southern Africa Region; former Chair, Department of Educational Communication and Technology, Kenyatta University, Kenya.

Rules for Re-engaging Community

Rule #1 – Boundaries connect as well as divide.

Rule #2 – Belonging is not fungible.

Rule #3 – Having “rights” is very different from belonging to a community.

Rule #4 – Distinguish beliefs from experience.

Rule #5 – All understandings are only partial.

Rule #6 – Uncomfortable is not unsafe.

Rule #7 – Distinguish between shame and guilt.

Rule #8 – Knowledge *for* not knowledge *of.*

Rule # 9 – Allow experience to precede judgement

Rule #10 – What we hold to be sacred, is usually non-negotiable

Rule #11 There is no monopoly on suffering

The Importance of Boundaries

Rule #1 – Boundaries connect as well as divide.

Boundaries are everywhere. Our bodies have their boundaries, and so do our property, the jurisdictional entities within which we carry out our business, our country, state, ethnic group, family, city, what we can tolerate, and what we can profess. We can find boundaries wherever we look. Even from this very short list, we can immediately see that some boundaries are hard and fast (legal jurisdictions) and some are fuzzy (boundaries of our ethnicity for example). Some boundaries are conceptual (what we can tolerate or profess, or for that matter of our love) and some are institutional (those of state power). Almost all of them are, at one time or another, in one form or another broached and so redefined, as are the entities they circumscribe.

Cities grow and incorporate what were once separate towns and villages across Africa. Ethnic groups come to include new members, as do families with every marriage. State power expands, and, at times, contracts as well. Thus, while boundaries have always existed and will always exist, their nature, relative permeability, flexibility, margins, and meanings change over time.

Think, for instance, about the tribal and ethnic boundaries across the continent. Whether one is Yoruba or Igbo in Nigeria, Zulu or Xhosa in South Africa, or Shona or Ndebele in Zimbabwe, or Luyha or Giriama in Kenya, ethnic identities remain deeply rooted in culture and tradition, but they are not static. Urban centres like Lagos, Nairobi, Johannesburg, Addis Ababa, and Accra have become melting pots of ethnicities, where boundaries of tribe, language, and even religion blur in the shared pursuit of work, education, and opportunity. Towns expand and welcome new settlers, inter-ethnic marriages become more common, and the forces of modernity, migration, and globalization reshape ancient divisions, challenging their rigidity. As cities grow, people increasingly live in diverse communities where the traditional markers of identity are less defined, and the boundaries that once kept groups apart become more fluid.

We cannot do without boundaries – whether of property, peoplehood, religion, or community – but nor can we cast them in immutable terms. Much of social life is all about negotiating boundaries: of right and wrong, of inclusion and exclusion, proper and improper behaviour, of our community and its traditions, of our people and its past and other peoples and their pasts. Our skin is another perfect example of a boundary that both separates and connects. Similarly, social boundaries – like those between clans or tribes – both create divisions and bring people into relationships. In Kenya when a Maasai warrior crosses into Kikuyu territory, the boundary between tribes becomes a bridge for trade, diplomacy, or even marriage.

From this, we can see that boundaries are extremely ambiguous entities. Ambiguous in terms of their permeability, in terms of their negotiability, their margins and meanings but also, we should note, in their very function: after all, boundaries both connect and divide. The boundary of our property both separates us from our neighbors but also connects us to them. We won't let our neighbour's fence encroach on our lawn, but gladly offer her a piece of pie across the fence. Our skin, the boundary of our body, separates us from the world around us but also connects us: whether in acts of love or physical hurt.

Thus, boundaries both separate and unite. The very act of distinguishing between one entity and another always also brings them in relation to one another. Boundaries thus point both outward as well as inward. They signify the world beyond as well as what is contained within. Think of the relationship between Kenya and its neighbouring countries. For decades, the borders between Kenya, Uganda, and Tanzania were open for trade, tourism, and migration. Yet, these boundaries have been tightened during times of tension. Examples include the fallout over disputed elections or during periods of heightened security concerns, like after the Westgate attack in 2013, and also during the COVID cases in 2020 and 2021. In Kenya's political life, boundaries have also, historically, played a dangerous role. The boundaries between ethnic groups have routinely been politicized during elections, most tragically during the post-election violence of 2007-2008. Boundaries that once allowed peaceful coexistence suddenly hardened, and neighbours turned against each other in some regions. Yet even here, after the violence, boundaries were re-negotiated. Communities that were displaced found ways to re-integrate, even though scars remained. The fluidity of these boundaries mirrors the fluidity of boundaries in human relations, where what separates can also unite and where conflict can turn into cooperation.

Boundaries are ambiguous in another way: they both constrain and are constrained by the power of their centre, that which provides the organizing force or principle of which they are the limit or margin. As limits or margins, boundaries share in the defining traits and characteristics of whatever field of meaning or significance they circumscribe, but they are also impinged upon by whatever lies beyond the field of such meaning. Hence their dangerous nature.

The very structure of our thinking mandates boundaries (through our use of categories, all of which have their limits or boundaries), but they are, at the same time, always a threat to the ways we think; precisely because they are at their limits and hence open to the impingement of other ways of thinking as well.

Perhaps the best example of this in contemporary Africa can be seen in the ongoing struggles around the recognition and place of the LGBTQ community in public life. Traditionally, Kenyan society operated with a very clear set of boundaries when it comes to gender and sexuality. These boundaries are rooted in deeply held cultural, religious, and social beliefs, where identities were often binary – male and female, heterosexual relationships the norm, and any divergence from these norms seen as an aberration. These boundaries have structured how people think about families, marriage, and even the concept of what it means to be a man or a woman. However, the visibility of LGBTQ individuals in Kenya has increasingly challenged these traditional boundaries. Their very existence confronts the categories that many people in Kenya have long taken for granted. Discussions around legal recognition for LGBTQ individuals, including their right to freedom of expression, equal treatment under the law, and access to healthcare, have brought the issue into the public sphere. In 2019, the High Court of Kenya upheld laws criminalizing homosexuality, reinforcing the legal boundaries that constrain the LGBTQ community. For many Kenyans, this judgment aligns with their cultural and religious understanding of gender and sexuality. For others, these laws represent outdated and oppressive boundaries that need to be redefined to reflect a more inclusive society.

This tension between the boundaries imposed by traditional beliefs and the push for inclusivity illustrates how boundaries are not fixed but constantly negotiated and contested. The boundaries that define gender and sexuality in Kenyan society are furthermore being impinged upon by global discourses on human rights and personal identity. LGBTQ individuals in Kenya are not only challenging the boundaries of legal recognition but also the very conceptual boundaries that have long defined Kenyan societal norms.

The ambiguity of boundaries is thus clearly evident. On one hand, they provide structure and a sense of order, helping people define their identity and place in the world. On the other hand, they are always open to challenge and reinterpretation, especially when confronted with individuals or ideas that do not fit neatly into established categories as in the case of the LGBTQ community. While boundaries are essential to how we think, organize society, and create meaning, they are also the sites of potential transformation. The very structure of our thinking mandates boundaries, but they are also constantly under pressure to change, particularly when they encounter other ways of thinking.

For these and other reasons, we often feel a certain degree of discomfort upon approaching our own boundaries and those of others. Ambiguous, they are dangerous as well. Something slippery we feel about boundaries, they are neither one thing nor the other, or perhaps are both and neither. Not only the trans-gendered athletes but also; the very light-skinned black woman who "passes" as white; the stranger who – as Georg Simmel taught us – comes today and stays tomorrow; the Jew who, as Shakespeare puts in the mouth of Shylock, will ... buy with you, sell with you, talk with you, walk with you, and so on; but [...] will not eat with you, drink with you, nor pray with you. Think of our in-laws: it is unclear if they are strangers or family, not quite either actually, which is what makes for occasional uncomfortable moments at family affairs.

The nature of boundaries changes over time, just as the balance of power shifts. In the early days of colonialism, boundaries were imposed by foreign powers, dividing ethnic groups into arbitrary territories across Africa. The infamous Berlin Conference of 1884–

85 saw European powers carve up the continent without regard for the cultural, ethnic, or social ties that predated colonial rule. For example, the Hausa and Fulani people, who once had fluid borders across West Africa, found themselves divided between what is now Nigeria, Niger, and other surrounding nations. Similarly, the Ewe people were split between modern-day Ghana and Togo by British and German colonial boundaries, the same happened to the Maasai who found themselves in Kenya and Tanzania.

These borders were not just lines on a map; they redefined how ethnic groups could move, trade, and live, restricting the freedom that had once been a hallmark of their societies. The struggle for independence across the continent—whether in Algeria, Ghana, Kenya, or Zimbabwe—was in part a struggle to reclaim the right to define what it means to be part of a nation, to reassert control over lands and identities that had been arbitrarily divided by colonial rule. The effects of these imposed boundaries continue to influence ethnic relations and national identities today.

Today, the power of the state in defining and maintaining boundaries can be seen in national debates over land ownership, political representation, and resource allocation. A good example is Lamu in Kenyan, where the national government's plans to develop a port and oil pipeline have created tensions with local communities. The boundaries between state power, local governance, and traditional land rights have come into sharp focus. Communities in Lamu argue that their ancestral land rights are being overlooked, while the government insists that national development projects take precedence. This conflict highlights how boundaries between local and national interests can clash and must be constantly negotiated.

We can also see the ambiguity of boundaries in personal identities as well, such as in the intergenerational tension within Kenyan families. Many young people today straddle the boundary between traditional cultural expectations and the globalized, modern world. A young Kikuyu girl from Nyeri may find herself negotiating the boundary between her family's traditional expectations of marriage and childbearing and her ambitions for education and career in Nairobi. These boundaries are not fixed but are constantly being redefined through negotiation, compromise, and sometimes conflict.

Thus, we note that boundaries are all around us and encompass too many cases, peoples and entities to be easily ignored. And we must remember that, as long as people have lived in communities (that is from time out of mind), there have been boundaries between these communities. The nature of these boundaries – their relative flexibility, porousness, the extent to which people could exist on their boundaries and so on – has not, however, been a historical constant. The historian Daniel Boyarin, in his important study *Border Lines*, analyzes the slow and highly negotiated process through which Christianity and Judaism split off into separate civilizational endeavours.

Kenya's history, for example, is full of examples of communities that have lived side by side, respecting and sometimes crossing each other's boundaries. In the pre-colonial era, the Giriama and the Swahili people of the Kenyan coast lived together with fluid boundaries. The Giriama farmed the land, while the Swahili controlled trade along the coast. Though different in culture and language, their economies were interdependent, and they often worked together, trading goods, marrying across boundaries, and sharing knowledge. This relationship was not without friction, but it was also marked by cooperation and mutual respect.

Boundaries are not just lines that divide people; they are spaces of interaction. Across Africa, communities have long used these spaces to foster trade, cultural exchange, and social cohesion. In cities like Johannesburg, South Africa, the neighbourhood of Hillbrow is a vibrant hub where people from across Southern Africa—Zimbabweans, Mozambicans, Malawians, and South Africans—live and work together. The area, once seen as a boundary of division, now reflects how nationality, ethnicity, and economic status are constantly negotiated and reshaped.

Similarly, in cities like Lagos, Nigeria, or Abidjan, Côte d'Ivoire, migrant workers from neighbouring countries have created bustling markets where local populations and foreign traders collaborate and interact daily. The borders of nationality, ethnicity, and religion are fluid in these spaces, reflecting how boundaries are not static but dynamic and flexible, adapting to the evolving needs and circumstances of those who live within them. These urban centers, much like Eastleigh's "Little Mogadishu" in Kenya, show how boundaries serve as zones of connection, where economic and social ties transcend rigid definitions of identity.

Boundaries both define the limits of group membership but are, at the same time, the point at which the group is exposed to outside forces and influences - hostile, seductive, enchanting, or threatening as the case may be. Boundaries must be defended, of this there can be no doubt. But they can also be crossed with more than tanks and armoured personnel carriers.

Boundaries divide us, and often that division is lethal. But they can also connect us, and that connection occurs, at least at first blush, more often than not, on the margins themselves. We may think here of the historical marginalization of the Nubian community who have lived in Kenya for over a century since their arrival as conscripts in the British colonial army. The Nubians have long occupied a space at the margins of Kenyan society—not fully outside, but never quite at the center either. While they were tolerated, they faced continuous struggles over land rights, identity, and legal recognition. This status placed them in a position of being "in-between"—neither fully rejected nor entirely accepted.

The Nubians' situation speaks to the nature of tolerance. Tolerance isn't about accepting all-out threats to our identity, nor is it about accepting individuals or groups who directly challenge the core of who we are. Instead, tolerance applies to those who exist at the edges of a society's definition of itself—those who live on the margins but do not threaten the heart of the collective identity. In Kenya, Nubians were largely tolerated, coexisting with other communities but always with a sense of uncertainty regarding their place in the nation. Today they contribute to the cultural tapestry of the country, especially in areas like Kibra where their influence is felt in both the history and social structures of the settlement.

One way to understand this development is to recognize how, the thicker the boundaries, the greater the number of individuals, behaviours and attitudes will reside on that boundary; the thinner that boundary, the fewer. Thick boundaries can encompass multiple types of difference, thin boundaries tend to be restricted and narrowly conceived. Thus, on June 2nd, 2017, the Kenyan government issued a community land title to the Nubian community trust for 288 acres of land in the Kibera neighbourhood of Nairobi, and so they have found a place within the "thick" boundaries of Kenyan society, living on the margins but slowly integrating through their established communities navigating complex negotiations of identity while retaining their cultural uniqueness. In fact, the thicker the communal boundaries, the more we are forced to define what we mean by "our" community as we will more and more come into contact with behaviours and beliefs that we find objectionable (without them necessarily threatening our identity, though perhaps causing us to make endless calculations as to the existence or non-existence of such a threat).

It is thus well to bear in mind that traditional societies which had strongly delineated group or communal identities (often of a primordial nature) were also societies with very thick boundaries, with very wide corporate identities and group definitions that necessitated some tolerance toward those who stood out by their difference from the majority culture. To some extent, these orientations and attitudes remain in place, in Kenya and Africa in general. While such tolerance is not always enacted, a tradition of enacted tolerance does run from Biblical injunctions on how to treat the stranger and sojourner through medieval (European) concerns with the terms of our duties to members of other religious communities. All of these stand in stark contrast to the situation in many countries today (where for example, American citizens who leave water in the deserts for illegal immigrants dying of thirst can be arrested).

In fact, today, in many European and North Atlantic societies, group identities have been replaced by individual identities, and the problem of tolerance of difference has been replaced by the legal recognition and entitlements of rights. In a sense, we may say that so-called modern societies have elided the problem of group identities and tolerance. They have replaced tolerance with rights. Of course, that leaves those "strangers", such as illegal immigrants who don't have many rights, quite beyond the pale: a fact whose horrific consequences can be seen in the USA, Europe, North Africa and elsewhere.

Thus, while perhaps there is nothing wrong (practically or morally) with "solving" the problem of communal boundaries by redefining them in purely individual terms the consequences for millions of individuals have been dire. For, it is always membership in a particular community that allows even bare existence. Existing beyond the confines of a community, refugees and immigrants have little recourse to the rights that are purportedly the province of all. Moreover, a glance at any newspaper would indicate that the conditions that defined the "high-modernity" of the Western European and North Atlantic nation-states—which valued the rights-bearing individual and so permitted the elision of the problem of communal boundaries—are currently changing. Return to group-based identities and religious commitments in many parts of the world, the growth of trans-national identities predicated on religion, race as well as ethnicity and nationhood not dependent on statehood, are all calling into question the type of individual identities that stood at the core of the revolutionary idea of citizenship.

Across Africa today, the politicization of group-based identities is an ongoing and dangerous development. Many post-independence nations sought to transcend tribal and ethnic boundaries in favour of national unity within the modern nation-state, but this ideal is increasingly under threat as ethnic and religious identities become more pronounced in political and social life. This phenomenon can be observed in numerous countries, where ethnic identity plays a critical role in shaping political outcomes and fueling tensions.

In Nigeria, for instance, electoral politics have often been deeply influenced by ethnic and regional divisions. The Hausa-Fulani, Yoruba, and Igbo ethnic groups have historically aligned themselves with different political factions, leading to tensions and periodic violence, particularly during elections. The Nigerian Civil War (1967–1970), driven in part by ethnic and regional tensions, continues to cast a long shadow over the country's politics. At the core are issues of marginalization and resource allocation often sparking conflict.

In Côte d'Ivoire, ethnic and religious identities have also been politicized, contributing to the civil wars of the early 2000s. The conflict between the largely Muslim north and the predominantly Christian south exacerbated divisions, leading to cycles of violence and political instability. Elections in 2010 resulted in widespread violence, as political allegiances were drawn along ethnic and religious lines.

In Ethiopia, ethnic federalism—introduced in the 1990s—was meant to accommodate the country's diverse ethnic groups, but it has also contributed to growing tensions. Recent conflicts between the Tigray, Amhara, and Oromo groups have shown how ethnic identities continue to shape political dynamics, often with devastating consequences for national unity.

These examples, much like the case of Kenya, reveal how tribalism and ethnic politics across Africa foster exclusionary identity politics, leaving little room for trust, openness, or tolerance beyond the boundaries of one's ethnic or religious group. The persistence of such divisions threatens social cohesion and national stability in many parts of the continent, as people increasingly align themselves with their ethnic communities rather than with a shared national identity.

We have therefore no choice but to re-engage with, even be willing to bump up against our boundaries, between individuals, communities, nation-states, peoples, languages, and racial groups. Attempts to short-circuit the problem by defining away the multitude of complex, often contradictory yet constitutive boundaries between us through the legal, political and philosophical doctrines of individual rights have come up short. For, as we shall shortly see, rights do not provide belonging nor is community simply an amalgam of rights-bearing individuals. To be in a community is more akin to being in communion and has nothing in common with exerting one's rights. Boundaries are not to be elided nor denied, but as we re-engage with them, we must continually bear in mind what may well be the first rule of communal living: Ultimately, boundaries define who we are, but they also challenge us to reach beyond who we are. They are the point at which we encounter the "other" – whether that is another person, another community, or another way of thinking. It is at these boundaries that we grow, negotiate, and sometimes find common ground. In Africa's rich mosaic of tribes, languages, and landscapes, boundaries are inevitable. But they are also the spaces where we learn to live with each other, to negotiate our differences, and to create something new.

Rule #1, Boundaries connect as well as divide

Application: Respect boundaries but be willing to bump up against them and even at times, cross them.

Group Reflection Prompts:

Act out the following scenes and spend time discussing the results of each:

- *Scene #1:* First, divide your group in two and make a boundary between them (how is up to you). Now try to think of how many different ways you can interact on/across/between/within this boundary. Do so. (Remember you can cross the boundary, but you cannot dismantle it).
- *Scene #2:* Again, divide the group in two and make a boundary between them. This time, however, also set up a third group of people whose job it is to maintain that boundary. Proceed with the activities you did in Scene #1 and see what happens.

Community and Belonging

Rule #2 – Belonging is not fungible.

There are many ways of describing or talking about community. And there are debates in anthropology and sociology on the meaning of community that go back well over 100 years. Let us stress here just one of its central aspects, that of belonging. It is now 70 years since Simone Weil wrote on the need for human belonging. In her words:

> *To be rooted is perhaps the most important and least recognized need of the human soul. It is one of the hardest to define. A human being has roots by virtue of his real, active, and natural participation in the life of a community which preserves in living shape certain particular treasures of the past and certain particular expectations for the future.*
>
> Observe this to be an inescapable truth.

To be rooted is to belong and to belong is to be a member of a community, a community with its own past, its own traditions, stories, smells, tastes, jokes, obligations, recipes, holidays, moral judgments, boundaries of what is permissible and prohibited, basic frames of meanings, fears, and desires. That is to say—and it is increasingly necessary to say it in no uncertain terms—it is to be a member of a *particular* community, with a particular past, particular stories, smells, tastes, and so on. It is not for an individual to merely pick and choose belonging. In many ways, this challenges much contemporary opinion, culture and "received knowledge" which sees belonging as fungible, intersectional and a function solely of individual choice. Such a perspective - influenced by Western individualism – stands in contrast to communities in Africa where belonging is deeply embedded in lineage and cultural practices, often determined by birth. In Kenya, a Kikuyu child born into the *Mbari ya Ngengi* (a clan) automatically belongs to that lineage, carrying its duties, privileges, and obligations. Many communities - the Luo, Luyha, Abagusii and Kamba - have a deeply rooted connection to their ancestral lands and origins. They hold a belief that true peace in death can only be achieved when one is buried on their family land, a sentiment expressed by elders even today.

Among the Yoruba communities of Nigeria, lineage and kinship ties are central to one's identity. Being born into a particular lineage or clan within the Yoruba tradition comes with specific roles, responsibilities, and rights that are inherited, not chosen. These roles might involve participation in ceremonies, leadership in religious or cultural rituals, or stewardship of family lands, which have been passed down through generations. Similarly, in Ethiopia, the Oromo people have a system called *gada*, a traditional system of governance where age sets determine leadership roles and social responsibilities within the community. Belonging to an age set and carrying out the obligations associated with it is a lifelong commitment, not something one opts in or out of. This system connects individuals to their community and history in ways that transcend modern notions of individualism.

Among the Shona people of Zimbabwe, the connection to ancestral land is deeply ingrained. The Shona beliefs hold that ancestors are the custodians of the land, and a person's identity is intrinsically tied to their place of birth. Returning to one's ancestral land for burial is seen as essential to maintaining the connection with one's forebears and ensuring spiritual continuity. This rootedness in land and lineage speaks to a form of belonging that is fixed in tradition and community, rather than individual choice.

In many African societies, this sense of belonging is non-negotiable and deeply tied to the community's historical, spiritual, and social fabric. Belonging is not simply interchangeable or fungible; it is inherited, lived, and transmitted across generations, making it a communal understanding that shapes the lives of individuals within the broader social order. Even in diverse, densely packed environments, (from Soweto South Africa to Kibra in Kenya, or Makoko in Lagos) people form micro-communities based on ethnicity, religious ties, or shared experiences of survival.

A Yoruba man living in Makoko still finds his sense of belonging tied not only to his immediate surroundings but also to his ancestral home in the southwestern region of Nigeria. Despite living in an urban slum, his identity remains connected to the customs, language, and traditions of his people. Similarly, in

Soweto, a Zulu or Sotho resident might navigate life in the city while maintaining strong ties to rural areas where their family and ancestral roots lie. In Nima, an informal community with people from various ethnic groups in Ghana, the same dynamic is visible. A Dagomba resident from northern Ghana may live in the heart of Accra, but their sense of belonging is tied not just to their urban neighbourhood, but also to the northern traditions, festivals, and communal obligations of their ethnic group. In Kenya, a Luo man living in Kibra might still find his sense of belonging tied not only to his immediate surroundings but to his ancestral home by Lake Victoria. His identity and community are defined not only by his immediate urban environment but also by the traditions and language of his people.

Belonging requires others and communities, which are not easily fungible. The story of the Mau Mau rebellion in Kenya, the circumcision rites of the Maasai, or the Luo mourning rituals after the death of a loved one are not interchangeable. Relations among the Kikuyu and Kalenjin are not the same as those among (or between them and) the Mijikenda. Attitudes of the Meru toward the Maasai are not comparable to those of the Luhya or the Taita.

Among the Luo, humour often involves satire and wit, reflecting their strong oral traditions, while among the Luhya, storytelling is a communal affair, rich with metaphors tied to farming and domestic life. A joke that might resonate deeply with a Kamba audience, steeped in the history of their resilience in the semi-arid regions of Kenya, may not land the same way with a Turkana listener. Humour, like other cultural expressions, is rooted in belonging to a specific community with its own shared experiences, Swahili coastal humour is different from that of the Kisii, and both again, from the jokes of the Kamba.

Moreover, and critically, these communities are circumscribed entities. These, our communities of belonging, are not universal but are bound by attributes that they consider unique, just as families are bound; they have their own histories and their own trajectories, their own languages and jokes, their own obligations and taken-for-granted worlds, their own flavours, and scents—their own understandings of home. They may be more or less open, more or less ascribed; their boundaries may be more or less permeable, but they do have boundaries which always define some "us" as against some "them". For, if boundaries are to include in any meaningful sense, they must also exclude. The terms of inclusion and exclusion are, often enough, subject to (sometimes violent) negotiation, historical change, redefinition, interpretation, and endless contestation. But exclude they must, however difficult this may be for many to accept, especially in relation to the contemporary hegemonic framing of human rights as universal and transcendent of all (group) boundaries.

For, at the end of the day, we cannot live without these communities of belonging and, despite all the dangers that arise from them, there is no possibility of human life or achievement outside of them. Again, this is not to say that such communities are an unalloyed good—they are not; often they are oppressive and restrictive—even if we discount their exclusionary character, which of course is the great bugbear of contemporary politics.

Thus, while community among Jews, Christians, Muslims, and others for that matter, is often a much-heralded virtue, bringing with it not only mutual concern, but mutual aid societies, hospitals, old-age homes, schools, charity organizations, burial societies, and much else, it is also, often enough, oppressive. Within certain communities, we may find an undo concern with what neighbours eat, how they dress, where they send their children to school, who they marry, and so on. Yes, to be sure, some communities are more restrictive than others—some define their boundaries in a more rigorous, ascriptive manner than others— but all are exclusive, as any group of people must be if it is to give full meaning to the terms of community. And it is precisely within these bounded communities—which are, moreover, real, and active entities— that human actors are born, thrive, live, die, and make sense (or do not) of their worlds and the worlds of others. Membership in the community remains an essential component of any shared vision of the good. It is not incidental that in East Africa when you ask people where home is, they tell you: "Where my ancestors are buried." This is true among many peoples in the world, though not so much among Western liberals, which is perhaps one reason for so many misunderstandings. Different homes, however, understand such matters as individual, community, terms of communal membership and so on very differently.

Let us remember that while belonging brings with it mutual aid, solidarity, and protection, it can also be oppressive. Communities may enforce norms that restrict individual freedom, like among the Kuria, where women's roles are strictly delineated by tradition, leaving little room for deviation. While belonging is an anchor for many, it also comes with costs—both personal and societal.

This is the truth that the French philosopher Simone Weil pointed out during the raging years of World War II and to which the political philosopher Hannah Arendt also drew our attention, pointing out that not only are individual rights embedded within political communities, but that while we can indeed leave any particular community with its obligations and moral ties, such an act can also only replace one set of ties with another—for life outside community is not possible.

Critical to a community's workings and role in sustaining human flourishing is the moral credit that is granted to its members. What we mean by moral credit is something colloquially phrased as affording someone the "benefit of the doubt." As our moral knowledge, social obligations, and sense of what is right and proper—as well as improper and destructive—is held collectively by us as members of specific social groups rather than by us solely as individuals, an important part of what it is we know is bound up with who we trust.

This is not an abstract notion but a bind in which we often find ourselves called upon to grant moral credit to some source in matters which are, by their nature, almost always morally ambiguous. We may not dispute any particular "fact" or "set of facts": the election of a governor in a contested county like Nairobi; the violent clashes during the 2007-2008 post-election period in Naivasha; the killing of a man suspected of cattle theft in Laikipia; the deployment of police forces in Mathare Nairobi, after a demonstration turned violent, or during a university students riot. However, the framing of these events, the set of relevant external bits of information, and the histories needed to explain them will often be shaped by the biases of our group belonging and the moral credit that we, as members of a community, grant to the source of such information. For instance, one need only think of the 2016 police shooting of a young man in Kisumu during post-election protests. All pieces of data may be factual—the man was a protester, the police were controlling a crowd—but it is often the biases of one's group of belonging that determine which descriptive elements are considered significant: was the man a protester seeking justice, or was he part of a violent mob? Was the police action justifiable or was it excessive force? Description in itself is always commentary and never plain fact.

Sometimes benign but increasingly less so, the claims of community and the need for belonging are challenging the liberal order of individual rights in untold ways and with as yet unknown consequences. The challenge is how to accommodate these claims without necessarily accepting the demands that often go with them—border walls, indifference to the fate of refugees and migrants, forced assimilation of immigrant communities, racist and ethnocentric policies that support authoritarian rulers, etc. How can we articulate a politics of belonging—which we recall, always embraces some exclusionary element—without succumbing to the rhetoric of the extreme right both at home and abroad? While continued advocacy of human rights may well be necessary, rights by themselves are far from a sufficient condition for human flourishing and the need for roots; a sense of belonging must be accommodated if we are to be spared a replay of some of the worst horrors of the last century.

Going one step further we note that communities of belonging are rooted in, particularity, the unique, the non-universal, and the non-generalizable. In fact, rootedness itself is a primary concern of communities of belonging. Communities of belonging provide for that fundamental human need for "rootedness." And to be rooted is to belong and to belong is, in turn, to be a member of a community. Belonging, rooted as it is in a particular community with a particular past, is necessarily a collective phenomenon. In the view of a community of belonging, the individual is only a distinct unit with reference to the larger community in which they belong. The individual belongs to and within the community. Thus, in communities of belonging, individuals are intertwined in complex networks of interconnection and interdependency. Autonomous, isolated individuals are illegible to a community of belonging. Further, individuals who belong, those rooted in particular places and times, are not generalizable and, therefore, not interchangeable. This sense of specialness is a large part of what makes belonging desirable.

The boundaries of such communities can be drawn in many different ways, some more fixed and impassable (such as those drawn according to supposedly ascriptive categories) and some more negotiable (like those mediated by traditions around religious conversion or intermarriage). Yet, in one way or another, the boundaries of a community of belonging are more often than not drawn around the entire collective. This means the boundaries are often thicker, in the sense discussed in our previous chapter. However, for that very reason, they also allow for more possibilities of play and negotiation to happen at their borders. Particular individuals may negotiate their relation to their own community of belonging as well as to others in various ways without having to make absolute or final claims.

We cannot live without these communities of belonging. Despite the dangers that may arise from them, they are integral to human life. In Kenya, this is evident in *Gikuyu oaths*, where sworn commitments to the land and to the ancestors guide many in the community's sense of justice and land rights. These practices, while deeply meaningful, can also become exclusionary. The Mau Mau struggle for land, independence, and justice was founded on communal belonging, but it also revealed the oppressive aspects of boundaries, where non-*Gikuyu* individuals were excluded from certain allegiances.

In Nigeria, the Fulani herders and sedentary farming communities often clash over land and water resources. The deep communal ties and ancestral claims to land among farming communities make these disputes particularly sensitive, as land ownership is tied not just to economic survival but to cultural identity and belonging. This sense of belonging, while meaningful, can become exclusionary, fueling conflicts between ethnic groups over rightful ownership and access to resources.

In South Africa, the ongoing debates about land reform and redistribution are another example of how communities of belonging shape contemporary social dynamics. Many Black South Africans view land restitution as a matter of ancestral justice, with claims to specific territories based on historical connections. The emphasis on communal belonging to the land is integral to identity, but it also complicates efforts to create inclusive solutions in a country still deeply divided by its apartheid history. The communal sense of entitlement to land can be both a source of solidarity and a point of tension, particularly when other groups feel excluded from these claims.

In Ethiopia, the ongoing ethnic conflicts in regions like Oromia and Tigray further illustrate the complexities of belonging. Ethnic-based federalism, where regions are largely divided by ethnicity, reinforces a sense of communal identity tied to land and governance. However, it has also led to exclusion and violence, as ethnic groups vie for control of resources and political power. The communal bonds that define belonging in these regions are strong, but they also highlight how boundaries, once reinforced by ethnic affiliation, can spark conflict.

In the Democratic Republic of Congo, ongoing tensions between the Hutu and Tutsi communities, exacerbated by regional conflicts and migration from neighbouring Rwanda, reveal similar dynamics. These groups have deep-rooted communal identities that are tied to both their historical presence in the region and their sense of belonging to larger ethnic networks. However, these identities have also become exclusionary in certain contexts, contributing to violence and instability.

Though these communities may open themselves to outsiders through conversion, intermarriage, or cooperation, boundaries still exist. These boundaries, whether rooted in language, tradition, or geography, form the essence of what defines "us" versus "them." The Samburu and Rendille of Kenya have shared land, culture, and practices, but the nuances that define each community remain intact, creating a distinction in their customs, traditions, and communal rites of passage, such as the *Samburu moran* initiation ceremonies.

We should add here that many existential conditions exercise a normative force on communities, regardless of their sense of belonging. The traditional practices of Kenyan communities often emphasize collective responsibility toward the vulnerable members of society. For instance, in the Kikuyu community of Kenya, there is a customary obligation known as *gucokia mburi* (returning a goat), which requires the community to care for the orphaned, the widowed, and the elderly by ensuring their needs are met. Similarly, many other Kenyan communities have long-held practices that mandate caring for those in vulnerable positions—just as the widow, orphan, and stranger hold a central place of obligation in the Bible. These responsibilities transcend any sense of belonging and are simply moral duties that bind the community together.

All of this is not to say that the costs of belonging are insignificant. Often, in order to remain within the bounds of a community of belonging, one must subsume his or her individual will and desires to the needs and tasks of the collective. This requires substantial discipline and self-sacrifice. However, for many people, rootedness within their community of belonging is integral to their sense of self and way of being in the world: forsaking their group on behalf of their individual desires, or in the name of individual rights, is a serious matter involving a fundamental reorientation of self. Thus, the movement from community to community, made possible by the regime of individual rights, also facilitates a change in the sense of self.

Finally, attending to the notion of moral credit, we can see an important difference between a community understood as a grouping of rights-bearing individuals and communities of belonging. Speaking in generalizations, communities of belonging tend to extend a certain amount of moral credit to their members simply on the basis of belonging to the same community. A member of the Buganda Kingdom in Uganda might more willingly trust a fellow Muganda over a Belgian United Nations official simply on the grounds of communal belonging. This moral credit extended to members of the community of belonging helps maintain cohesion within the community amidst changing or challenging circumstances. It also contributes to the feeling of belonging itself: I know I belong because I am extended moral credit. However, of course, an extension of this credit may be more-or-less well-founded in any particular case. The UN official may turn out to be operating in good faith while your fellow Muganda could be a swindler. However, the phenomenon maintains its importance as a human social fact that should not be overlooked.

In communities of rights-bearing individuals, however, in theory, moral credit has little public role. Individuals are evaluated on an individual basis. In such a view attributing credit (or blame) to people based on their membership in a certain community of belonging is considered a violation of the norms of formal justice. Still, the continuing realities of racism, sexism, Islamophobia, anti-Semitism, and white supremacy, to name just a few operative dimensions of collective judgment, demonstrate just how pervasive the extension and denial of moral credit on the basis of membership, real or perceived, in certain communities of belonging.

Even more interestingly, moral credit, or the benefit of the doubt granted to community members, plays a significant role in many societies. Among the Bukusu of Kenya, a strong sense of trust is given to community members, especially within their traditional initiation rites like circumcision ceremonies, where moral credit is extended based on a shared heritage. An outsider cannot easily earn this trust. But moral credit can also be challenged or withheld. Thus, for example, the tension in Marsabit County of Kenya, where longstanding issues between the Borana and Gabra communities sometimes flare into violence. Here, membership in a particular group can determine which version of the truth one believes, showing how the moral credit extended within communities also fosters biases.

And, finally, the moral credit so extended or denied is, to a great extent, tied to one overwhelming characteristic of such communities of belonging: that they are not fungible. That one can (and sometimes does) change one's community does not for all that, make them interchangeable.

Rule #2, Communities are not fungible.

Application: Accept exclusion as an aspect of inclusion and not always as an act of oppression.

Group Reflection Prompts: We have discussed community mostly in terms of belonging and the element of trust and moral credit that we grant to community members (as opposed to strangers). We have also pointed out that often too strong an emphasis on human rights as the sole vision of social organization fails to recognize this, critical, aspect of community. Belonging, however, is not the only aspect of life in a community. Therefore, following this reflection, we would like you to discuss together a number of questions regarding aspects of life in a community:

- What is the role of law in general and authority in particular to the meaning of community?
- How can a community accommodate difference (of individuals and sub-groups) and still remain a community of belonging?
- What is the difference between a community and a family, a clan, a tribe, a nation, or a religion?
- What is the role of a shared past in the making of a community of belonging?
- How can a newcomer join a community of belonging?

Belonging and Rights

Rule #3 - Having "rights" is very different from belonging to a community.

In the past 50 years, the rhetoric of human rights has grown increasingly prevalent in political discourse, visions of international cooperation, and the legitimation of a liberal international order. It has also redefined the rhetoric and thought of the "left" in advanced capitalist countries. Arguments for working-class solidarity have increasingly given way to heated advocacy of individual rights and an "identity politics" predicated on multiculturalism and the need for "recognition".

A "politics of rights," which were first advanced as an alternative to what many in the 1960s saw as the threat of global communism—especially in view of of the anti-colonial struggles of this era in Africa and elsewhere—succeeded beyond the wildest dreams of its advocates. The individual triumphed. Later, against the backdrop of the fall of the Soviet Union and its satellite states, and the rise of anti-democratic politics in many newly liberated African polities, the rhetoric (and concrete politics) of rights came to redefine what many thought of as "the liberal left" in the decades since 1989.

Liberalism had triumphed as a philosophical project and political agenda. At the time, however, the unintended consequences of this triumph were not even dimly perceived by its advocates, and it continues to be ignored by far too many who unquestioningly accept the individual unit of human rights as a self-apparent virtue.

By making human rights the highest and most noble of our social and political virtues, liberalism has all too often denied, denigrated, or simply turned a blind eye to other, equally significant visions of the human good, one particularly salient one being the need for belonging. To be rooted in a community, a way of life and a sense of place and purpose, beyond our immediate individual desires and wants, is a central aspect of the human experience in the world. In the words of Simone Weil: *This participation [in the life of a community] is a natural one, in the sense that it is automatically brought about by place, conditions of birth, profession and social surroundings. Every human being needs to have multiple roots. It is necessary for him to draw well-nigh the whole of his moral, intellectual, and spiritual life by way of the environment of which he forms a natural part.*

To ignore – or more forcibly deny - the need for these roots, and the participatory life with others that they create, is to denigrate a critical aspect of what it has always meant to be human. Further, while perhaps few would advocate for such explicitly, the current Western liberal focus on articulating human needs and obligations primarily in terms of rights does tend, very much, to blind us to these dimensions of our existence.

To give local examples from across Africa: In a Kenyan rural village, when a neighbour's house burns down, the community does not wait for government relief to assist. Instead, they quickly rally together to rebuild the house, offering materials, labour, and food. This help is offered not because the victim has a "right" to it, but because of the deeply ingrained sense of belonging and shared responsibility in the community. Everyone in the village is part of a mutual safety net built on long-standing relationships and trust, far beyond the logic of formal rights.

In rural Senegal, when a farmer's crops fail due to drought or other hardships, the surrounding community comes together to provide food, seeds, and labour to help the farmer get back on their feet. This communal support isn't driven by the farmer's "right" to aid but by the deeply held cultural value of *teranga* (hospitality and mutual support). In Senegalese communities, there is an unspoken agreement that everyone shares responsibility for each other's welfare, ensuring that no one is left behind in times of need.

In the communal traditions of the Igbo people in Nigeria, when someone in the village faces a crisis, such as the loss of a family member or a health emergency, the community swiftly organizes help—whether it's through financial contributions, emotional support, or communal labour. This solidarity is driven by a sense of belonging and the shared history that ties everyone together, not by formal legal obligations or rights. It is the moral and cultural fabric of the community that ensures individuals in distress are supported. Similarly, in Ethiopia, the concept of *Debo* (communal labour) is still practiced in rural areas. When a family needs help with building a house or harvesting crops, neighbours come together to assist, driven by the expectation that the favour will be returned in the future, not by any formal rights-based system.

In these examples, the help offered within African communities is based on trust, cultural values, and a shared sense of belonging, rather than on formalized "rights" frameworks. This contrasts sharply with more individualistic, rights-based systems, where assistance is often conditional on proving eligibility or entitlement. The African communal approach fosters an interconnectedness that transcends the need for formal recognition of rights, creating a mutual safety net embedded in everyday social life. These African examples contrast sharply with more impersonal, rights-based assistance programs, which often require the victim to prove their entitlement to aid.

The worlds of belonging and rights contain very different values, are suggestive of very different sentiments and are predicated on very different sociological conditions, conceptions of the other, ideas of fairness, mutuality, and understandings of community. Comparing these different dimensions of existence, we can highlight just how different these worlds are.

Belonging	**Rights**
Shared dispositions	Multicultural values
Moral community	Community of rights bearers
Value of peace/mercy	Value of justice
Familiarity	Strangeness
Sameness	Difference
Shared moral dispositions	Disparate moral values
Shared experience	Dissimilar experience
Moral credit granted to members	No credit granted, knowledge demanded
Others experienced as a risk.	Others experienced as a danger.
Trust between members	Confidence measures required of all

Risk leaves room for doubt	Danger requires security
Social bonds	Legal entitlements
Traditions and customs	Universal standards
Intrinsic value of relationships	Instrumental value of agreements
Organic trust-building	Regulatory frameworks
Historical continuity	Institutional structures
Forgiveness and reconciliation	Legal accountability and punishment
Collective responsibility	Individual responsibility
Cultural cohesion	Legal pluralism
Intergenerational continuity	Short-term contractual relations

In Kenya, this distinction is especially clear in situations of communal land ownership among pastoralist communities such as the Maasai. Belonging to the community grants access to communal resources like grazing lands and water, not because of any legal right but because of the mutual trust and social obligations members share. When drought strikes, the rights of the community members are not adjudicated through courts or government officials; rather, elders negotiate the use of resources based on social bonds and shared survival strategies developed over generations. This contrasts with urban areas where formal property rights often lead to disputes and court battles, especially among displaced families in slum settlements.

As we can see, rights provide no sense of belonging, appeal to no sentiment of shared community, and eschew the obligations entailed by already existing ties. In Nairobi's informal settlements, we often witness the growing gap between community-organized initiatives like *chamas* (informal savings and credit groups) that offer members both economic and social support, and the formal rights-based approaches to poverty alleviation. The *chama* system thrives on trust, belonging, and reciprocity, where each member's welfare is intimately linked to the well-being of the group. Government-driven initiatives, by contrast, often reduce individuals to beneficiaries of aid, stripping away the deeper social bonds and commitments that drive community cohesion.

The increasing divergence between confidence (in the "truths" we hold about the other) and trust (in their good-will), between reason and empathy, justice, and mercy—that is, between the claims of justice and those of a moral community —is one of the most challenging of all issues facing us today. The right side of our chart which represents confidence, security, and abstract justice, with the other assumed to be dangerous—is one of individual rights bearers, whose boundaries are sheer and absolute with but the thinnest of margins. The left side of our chart, which on the other hand is defined by trust and moral credit, where peace is the supreme value—is to a large extent a social space constituting wide margins and thick boundaries, where a good deal of discomfort, occasioned by actions on the boundary of the community, is "tolerated" precisely because individuals are seen as essentially part and parcel of one's own ideas of self.

One could well argue that such claims to communal mutuality can be made only when some minimal rule of law is already in place. And that may indeed be so. But it does not change the reality of people's need for belonging, a need to live among those with whom help is not understood in terms of legalized assistance programmes doled out by cold, bureaucratic, impersonal organizations and welfare agencies, but rather as arising out of a sense of personalized mutuality and shared life.

These communities are more and more being understood as walled enclaves—in the USA for Trump supporters; in Israel for supporters of Netanyahu and extreme right-wing parties, Italian supporters of Fratelli d'Italia, supporters of Orban in Hungary; as well as in many of the former Soviet bloc Eastern European states where the "iron curtain" built to keep citizens in, is being replaced with new, even higher razor-wired fences to keep immigrants and refugees out. And while these developments are a matter of no small concern, arguments for human rights do not properly address the problem; they exacerbate it.

In Africa as well, increasingly no-go zones are established from Kenya to South Africa – in areas where members of minority tribes or outsiders are evicted by more dominant ones and where the vision of pan-African solidarity has given way to both physical and metaphorical walled enclaves between communities. Ethnic and religious identities become markers of exclusion in Nigeria as in Côte d'Ivoire as long-standing historical, socio-economic, and political dynamics fuel distrust and competition between communities. What transpires in Africa is but one instance of what is sadly a global process.

The "bifurcation" of our social world, as presented in the foregoing table, into the worlds of belonging and rights, is of course an abstraction. The truth is not that we live in two universes but in many more. The real problem, however, is that the first world of trust and moral community of mercy and to speak somewhat poetically of "gifts" is predicated on sameness, on familiarity, and our assumptions of knowledge of the "other"—who, of course, is no longer an-other once she is known. That sameness, however, is always illusory—always partial, incomplete, and given to disruption. Nothing in the world is really "the same"; even snowflakes, we are told, are each different from one another in small ways.

Consequently, if we predicate our moral community on sameness—even liberal sameness—we will always be disappointed. We will always find one group or another existing somewhere on the margins of this "sameness" whom we will see as traitors who violate our shared moral code and reveal their true colours of strangeness and difference, especially in times of trial and tribulation. We will always fall into what Sigmund Freud called the "narcissism of the small difference" and so continually produce another, against whom to define our own sameness. At this point, the near other, he or she who is similar in so many ways but not in that one attribute, whatever it may be, achieves iconic standing as representing all that is different and threatening and therefore must be destroyed.

As long as trust is restricted to those who are the same, we will continually be patrolling the borders of this sameness to check for deviations and differences. The boundaries will be points of continual contention, fear, and opprobrium. In times of crisis like the terrorist attacks in Kenya by the Al-Shabaab, a similar pattern of suspicion and exclusion can be observed and the subsequent security crackdowns on certain communities, particularly in the coastal and northeastern regions, where there is a significant Muslim population. Following major attacks in Kenya, such as the Westgate Mall attack in 2013, the Garissa University attack in 2015, and other smaller-scale bombings, communities perceived to have even a slight association with the attackers – primarily ethnic

Somalis and Kenyan Muslims – were often subjected to suspicion, increased scrutiny, arbitrary arrests and harassment of Muslim citizens, particularly young men, by security forces. Areas like Eastleigh in Nairobi, which has a large Somali population, became synonymous with raids and crackdowns, and individuals from this community were often viewed as potential threats, regardless of their actual involvement in any criminal activity.

In Nigeria, after major Boko Haram bombings or kidnappings, including the abduction of the Chibok girls in 2014, Nigerian security forces have been known to conduct widespread raids in areas perceived to have Boko Haram sympathizers. Innocent civilians, particularly young men, have been arbitrarily arrested, and entire communities in the northeastern states have been profiled and treated as potential threats.

In Mali, where the rise of jihadist groups like Jama'at Nasr al-Islam wal Muslimin (JNIM) and al-Qaeda in the Islamic Maghreb (AQIM) has led to widespread violence, entire ethnic groups, such as the Fulani, have faced increased suspicion. Because some jihadist fighters hail from the Fulani community, this has led to counterinsurgency operations that target Fulani civilians, who are often wrongly assumed to be collaborators with terrorist groups.

This shift in perception parallels the phenomenon where those who are "a bit different" – in this case, Muslims and ethnic Somalis – began to be viewed as fundamentally "not like us" and therefore dangerous. Instead of leveraging the shared sense of belonging and community among Africa's diverse ethnic and religious groups, the state often invoked security laws, using the apparatus of justice and law enforcement to patrol these boundaries of difference. This exacerbated divisions and deepened suspicions, mirroring the way Jewish communities in Europe were treated in past centuries and how Muslim citizens are now viewed in certain European contexts. The result was a fragmented social fabric, where those seen as slightly different were no longer trusted, but instead perceived as threats to national security.

While there are no easy solutions to living with others, we must meet the challenge head-on in the form of developing a new politics of difference. Eschewing both the hard and impenetrable boundaries being set up by nationalist politicians between "us" and any manner of "them", as well as the ultimately homogenizing politics of abstract human rights that makes every individual a morally autonomous agent devoid of inherited ties and obligations; we propose instead a rigorous engagement with communal differences. To do so, we must appreciate the implications of trust and confidence and reorient our approach to boundaries, neither seeking to do away with, privatize, or absolutize them. We must come to see that boundaries do not only divide between an "us" and a "them", but rather distinguish among "us" as we really are. Embracing difference, as so many advocates of multiculturalism profess, is most probably impossible; for most of us, it is difficult enough to embrace our own traditions and pasts with their morally complex and compromised heritage. Living with difference is something else, however, and is indeed possible. But doing so necessitates the creation of new social and cognitive spaces, or better, places. Lest one thinks that this can be done digitally, it cannot. It must rather be lived in the full embodied sense of the term.

Thus, rather than create spaces of assimilation or segregation, we must construct places for difference—in the military, in schools, workplaces, religious institutions, and social arena where difference is encountered, wrestled with, and sometimes fought over. Only in this way can a shared language—which does not imply agreement or shared meaning—and thus civil politics come to be.

Rule #3 – Having "rights" is very different from belonging to a community.

Application: Recognize that sometimes a sense of belonging may be more important to people than "realizing" their rights.

Group Reflection Prompts:

- Tell a story about a time when you felt you truly belonged in a group. How does it feel to belong? How did you know you belonged?
- Tell a story about a time when you resisted the demands of your community of belonging. Why did you resist? On what grounds?
- Tell a story about a time you felt like your rights were denied or unfairly administered. How did this affect your sense of membership in the community?

- Tell a story about a time when you appealed to your rights to accomplish something. Were your rights respected? Were they ignored? How did this affect your relationships with those of whom you demanded your rights?

Strangers and Neighbours

Rule #4 – Distinguish beliefs from experience.

Who is a stranger, and who is a neighbour? More importantly, what are our obligations to each?

The answer to these questions today is much more complicated than in the past. In traditional African communities, boundaries of kinship, clan, and ethnic group were well-defined, and obligations to each were clear. The neighbour was often someone from the same clan, ethnic group, or village, and strangers were typically outsiders whose presence required careful negotiation. In many African communities, this dynamic is still visible today, especially in rural areas where proximity often translates into shared responsibility.

Within these communities, there exists a high degree of mutuality, shared values, and experiences in everyday activities such as fetching water from the communal river, going to market days, attending church services, or participating in clan meetings. A clear example can be found among the Luhya communities of Western Kenya, where neighbours assist each other in farming activities, constructing mud houses, and performing ceremonies like circumcision rites and marriage rituals. This neighbourly support crosses household lines, regardless of socio-economic status, and is deeply rooted in shared history and cultural values. For instance, during farming seasons, it is common for neighbours to come together to help each other in weeding or harvesting maize fields, with the understanding that they will reciprocate the favour. Additionally, neighbours often come together to build a house for someone in the community through *obulala* (a communal construction process). Even in moments of sorrow, such as during funerals, neighbours automatically step in to cook, clean, and comfort the bereaved family, without the expectation of reward.

These actions create a sense of solidarity and belonging. However, just as there is neighbourly support, there can also be rivalries and conflicts — whether over land disputes or boundary conflicts between farms. Despite these disagreements, the sense of communal belonging prevails. Even after a quarrel, the same neighbours will still meet at the local church or on the market days, often reconciling through the intervention of elders or clan leaders.

In Uganda, particularly among the Baganda people of the central region, a strong sense of community and mutual support is embedded in daily life and cultural practices. The concept of *bulungi bwa nsi* (communal work) exemplifies this. Neighbours come together to participate in activities such as clearing roads, digging wells, or cleaning communal spaces. This is done for the collective good, with each individual contributing to the welfare of the entire village or community. The Baganda community also have a strong tradition of mutual assistance in agricultural work, especially during tilling, planting and harvesting seasons. Families will organize *ekibina*, a rotational work group, where each household takes turns hosting the group to help with farming tasks, such as tilling land or harvesting crops like bananas and coffee.

Additionally, the Baganda community exhibits a deep commitment to supporting each other during life events such as weddings, funerals, and cultural ceremonies. For instance, during funerals, it is customary for community members to contribute towards the funeral arrangements through a process known as *okusonda,* where people offer financial or material support to the bereaved family. Women gather to cook meals for the mourners, while men take responsibility for organizing the burial rites. Despite occasional disputes over land or family inheritance, the sense of communal obligation ensures that conflicts are often resolved through dialogue, overseen by clan elders, who maintain peace and uphold the traditional values of the community.

Today, in many places, our feelings of connection to others and the obligations associated with such connections are much more diverse, perhaps spread thinner, but in any case, certainly wider and are not bounded by the physical space of neighbourhoods. Think of the power of crowdsourcing to get a sense of this change. In fact, with cell phones and social media, ties between people stretch across oceans and continents and many feel more connected, feel that they share more, with a distant ideological compatriot than with their immediate neighbours.

Moreover, in more urbanized and cosmopolitan parts of Africa such as Nairobi, Kigali, Kampala, Harare or Abuja, neighbours can sometimes be strangers. We may live in apartment blocks or estates where we hardly interact with the people next door. The idea of *harambee* (pulling together) that once defined the neighbourhood in Kenya has given way to individualism, as people's primary concerns stretch beyond the immediate vicinity. In places like Westlands or Lavington in Nairobi Kenya, Banana island or Ikoyi in Lagos, Nigeria and Cantonments or East Legon in Accra Ghana, it is not uncommon for people to live side by side for years without ever really knowing each other. Our connections are not defined by physical proximity but by broader social or professional networks. These networks, while important, often leave us disconnected from those we share space with in our daily lives.

In many ways, this change can be viewed as a "positive" development. Thanks to technology and social media, we can build and maintain relationships across regions, nations, and even continents. Many young Africans now have stronger ties to virtual communities based on shared professional or political interests than to the people living next door. For example, someone living in Nairobi, Kenya may feel more connected to a social media friend in London who shares similar views and orientations (political, cultural, aesthetic, or other) than they do to the elderly neighbour who lives across the street.

Yet, a cost is nevertheless extracted. We no longer feel the simple force, obligations, and mutuality of neighbourliness. Not to mention the fact that our ideological or professional associate from afar will not come to help when our roof leaks during the long rains, nor will they attend our family *harambee* to raise funds for a medical emergency. In traditional African society neighbours, even those we don't particularly care for, do this all the time.

As our neighbours have become strangers to us, our obligations to the stranger — a concept deeply ingrained in African culture — have diminished. Obligations to the stranger are ancient. In pre-colonial Kenya, many communities held to customs that protected strangers. For example, the Luo concept of *juok* or spirit protectors traditionally extended care and hospitality to travellers passing through their land, providing them with food and shelter. Among the Bantu-speaking communities in Southern Africa, for instance, the *Ubuntu* philosophy emphasizes interconnectedness and mutual care, where a stranger is seen not as a threat but as a guest deserving of respect, food, and shelter. Similarly, the Fulani people, spread across West Africa, practice *pulaaku*, a code that stresses generosity and the obligation to assist travellers. This is a long-standing tradition among Fulani households, where strangers are provided with sustenance and protection without question. Among the Maasai of Kenya and Tanzania, it has always been customary to welcome travellers by offering milk or meat as a sign of hospitality. For the Maasai, helping strangers strengthens communal bonds, fostering a sense of trust even with those from outside their group. Likewise, in Northern Ghana, the Dagomba people have a cultural expectation that strangers will be received by the village chief and offered food and shelter as a sign of goodwill. The Igbo of Nigeria also hold a deep sense of obligation to strangers, reflected in their saying *"Nwanne di na mba"* (a brother exists in every land), which expresses their tradition of caring for those far from home. Similarly, Somali pastoralists practice *martisoor*, offering travellers and refugees protection and shelter, ensuring they are treated as guests in times of need. These traditions highlight how African societies, across the continent, have long recognized the importance of providing care to strangers, reinforcing a communal ethic that goes beyond individual obligation.

Today, however, the boundaries between strangers and neighbours are blurred. In Kenya, Nairobi's Eastleigh neighbourhood, where a large Somali refugee population has settled, the concept of stranger and neighbour is continually being negotiated and renegotiated. Somali refugees are often regarded with suspicion by their non-Somali Kenyan neighbours, leading to tensions. Yet, in other instances, the same Somali refugees have become neighbours who contribute significantly to the local economy. Thus, a sense of mutual obligation is emerging, albeit imperfectly, with shared interests beginning to override ethnic and national differences.

This dynamic mirrors the biblical injunction in Exodus 12 that commands: "there shall be one law for the native and for the alien who resides among you." This command resonates with Kenyan religious communities, both Christian and Muslim, for generations. For example, during the post-election violence of 2007-2008, many church groups in Nairobi's Mathare slums opened their doors to neighbours fleeing ethnic violence, regardless of their ethnic identity. Similarly, Muslim clerics in Mombasa have urged their congregants to welcome non-Muslims into their homes during times of crisis, reflecting a long-standing tradition of hospitality. This sense of shared responsibility is also reflected in the traditions of West African Islamic communities. For example, in Senegal, the Mouride Brotherhood, a Sufi Muslim order, has a long tradition of providing sanctuary and aid to those in need, regardless of their religious or ethnic background. During times of political unrest or natural disasters, members of the brotherhood consistently open their doors to strangers, offering food, shelter, and spiritual support. Similarly, in Northern Nigeria, during the Boko Haram insurgency, local Muslim communities, particularly in cities like Maiduguri, have sheltered Christian refugees fleeing violence, despite the religious differences between them. These acts of solidarity show how the ancient ethic of hospitality toward strangers continues to influence social dynamics in contemporary Africa, ensuring that care and protection are extended to all, regardless of their background.

This is not to say that there are no complications in this ethic of mutuality with strangers. Thus, a neighbour in Kenya, whether in a rural village or an urban estate, owes their fellow neighbours certain considerations based on their shared membership in the community. But when it comes to strangers—such as refugees, immigrants, or individuals from different ethnic groups, different factors begin to play a role.

Legally, refugees like those in Dadaab or Kakuma camps are required to follow the laws of Kenya, just as citizens do. They may not have the right to vote or hold certain privileges granted to citizens, but they are still expected to adhere to the legal framework, including laws on taxation if they engage in economic activities.

The moral question, however, goes beyond legal obligations. Should these refugees or other non-citizens be integrated into the community in the same way as local neighbours? Should they be invited to contribute to local development projects, or receive the same communal support during times of need, such as during funerals or local ceremonies? For instance, if a Somali refugee from Dadaab participates in local markets or engages in trade with Kenyan citizens, does this economic engagement translate into a social obligation to the local community, or does their status as a "stranger" exempt them from such responsibilities?

In many cases, the moral and social obligations to strangers vary depending on local traditions and community values. Some communities might embrace refugees, seeing them as fellow human beings deserving of support and protection, while others may view them with suspicion, limiting the extent to which they can belong. The question of whether strangers should be held to the same codes of conduct, frame of obligations and understandings of mutuality or whether their differing cultural and moral values should be tolerated remains a subject of ongoing debate, and one that deeply reflects the tensions between legal belonging and communal identity in contemporary Kenya and elsewhere.

A neighbour owes their fellow neighbours a certain degree of consideration as a condition of their shared membership in the neighbourhood. Whether or not the stranger deserves this same consideration from the group, whether or not they should bear the same privileges and obligations, however, is an open question. Should strangers be held to the same standards to which members of the group are held? Should strangers be similarly sanctioned when they do not live up to them? Or, as outsiders, should strangers' differing moral evaluations be tolerated? Do the moral responsibilities of care inherent to neighbours, to members of the group, extend to the strangers existing on the group's boundaries? How one settles these questions has much to do with the communities of which one is a part and the traditions and authorities those groups observe.

For there is no doubt that the stranger, if included, changes the group in some way, and therein lies the problem. As an agent of change, the stranger may be met by a range of responses from the group. The group may welcome change, they may accept it, tolerate it, fear it, reject it, suppress it, or react in any number of other ways. Or all of these together. Change is ambiguous, and when communities encounter ambiguity, any number of responses is possible.

In Kenya's Laikipia County, where nomadic pastoralists from different communities (Turkana, Samburu, Maasai, and Kikuyu) have traditionally coexisted, the arrival of new herders from outside the region has led to tensions over grazing land. Some locals view these outsiders as strangers whose presence threatens the delicate balance of the ecosystem. The response from the community varies, however, as others have welcomed these strangers with a spirit of shared suffering due to droughts, while others have reacted with hostility, viewing them as competitors for scarce resources.

This illustrates the complexity of including strangers, whose presence may provoke a range of responses from welcome to fear. In Burkina Faso, a similar dynamic has unfolded between the Mossi farmers and the Fulani pastoralists. Traditionally, these communities have coexisted, with the Fulani moving their cattle across Mossi lands during seasonal migrations. However, in recent years, increased pressure on land due to population growth, climate change, and resource scarcity has strained this relationship. As Fulani herders, often displaced from other regions by droughts and conflicts, migrate in search of grazing land, they are sometimes met with hostility from Mossi farmers who fear for their crops and resources. While some Mossi villages continue to honour the traditional practice of offering pasture and water to the Fulani, others view the incoming herders as threats to their livelihood, leading to tensions and occasional conflict.

This situation highlights the delicate balance between hospitality and competition for resources, a theme that resonates across many African communities dealing with environmental and social pressures. Seeking to live together differently, that is to live with strangers, raises the following questions: Does turning the stranger into a neighbour necessarily imply eliminating the stranger's differences in order to assimilate them into the group? Must the stranger become like the group, must they convert, in order to have a life amongst the group? Or must the group give up its distinctiveness to incorporate the stranger? Neither of these options allows the option of preserving the differences of each. These dilemmas are not hypothetical. They are played out daily in places like Africa's urban slums, where diverse communities live side by side, sharing space but not always sharing values or experiences. The Congolese refugee living next door to a Luhya family in Kawangware, Kenya, must navigate a complex web of belonging and exclusion. Mutual accommodation is not a given but something to be negotiated daily.

We live in a global, mobile, and increasingly interconnected world. Encountering strangers in a globalized economy is unavoidable. We encounter strangers regularly. Thus, living amongst new and changing conglomerations of strangers, we are continually challenged by the demands of hospitality, whether as providers or recipients. What do our religious, moral, or political communities teach about encountering strangers? What resources for tolerance exist within our religious, moral, and political traditions to deal with the stranger? Can we live with their differences, even as they live amongst us? Living at peace in a world populated by different people with different political ideas, moral traditions, religious commitments, and communal loyalties requires that we answer these questions. And it may very well require the formation of different kinds of neighbourhoods, neighbourhoods where difference is not conflated with danger, but accepted, negotiated, and navigated with the goal of living together always in mind.

Rule #4 – Distinguish beliefs from experience._

Application: Accept our differential obligations to both neighbours and strangers, though we do have obligations to each.

Group Reflection Prompts:

- Tell a story about a time when you were a stranger in another community or country. How did you feel? How were treated?
- Tell a story about a time when a neighbour helped you. Do you think this same help would have been extended to a stranger in your community?
- How are strangers treated in your community?
- What do your communities of belonging say about the ways strangers should be treated?
- How does your community differentiate between strangers and neighbours?

Trust is not Confidence

Rule #5 – All understandings are only partial.

We often use the terms confidence and trust interchangeably. We treat them as synonyms. Yet much can be gained by parsing the difference. This difference between trust and confidence connects as well to another set of definitions we deal with in this section, that between risk and danger. Let us look at the difference between both terms, which will help us to understand something of relevance to our social interactions – especially our interactions with strangers and those who are different from us.

Confidence is based on knowledge of what will be and hence on our ability or assumed ability to predict another person's behaviour (which one could foresee in either positive or negative light). This knowledge may, in turn, be based not only on a system of either positive or negative sanctions (what grounds most market exchange) but also on what we may term familiarity.

We may use the example of football. Because Jabulani over there played football for Bafana Bafana with his friends in South Africa as a boy, he shares with me certain codes of conduct, certain moral evaluations, and certain ways of being and acting that bring me to have confidence in him. We are alike, the same, and hence I can predict his actions in a wide field of activities.

Knowledge of what will be, confidence and prediction, are here based not on sanctions but on sameness, on familiarity, on knowledge (or assumed knowledge) of how alter will act. Mind you, the relevant other may not be "the same" at all, but we will often draw certain conclusions (true or false) from modes of dress, speech, where he went to school, neighbourhood, religion and so on. All of this will allow us to construct a story of sameness that will in turn allow us to have confidence in our ability to predict behavior.

In the African context, this knowledge often comes from familiarity with shared social structures, like clan affiliations, religious practices, or ethnic ties. For instance, in many parts of Africa, members of the same ethnic group or clan often feel a sense of confidence when interacting with one another, based on shared cultural practices, norms, and expectations. In Kenya, a Giriama elder, for example, may have confidence in another Giriama man based on their shared upbringing in the same region, their similar family structures, or the fact that they belong to the same age set group. This is the same in Uganda or Mali.

This sense of predictability—this confidence—is reinforced by many shared experiences. For example, when a Maasai man from Kenya meets another Maasai from Tanzania, their common cultural heritage allows them to predict each other's actions, such as how they will participate in the *Enkipaata* (age-set initiation ceremonies) or behave in communal negotiations over grazing land or even a simple act of greeting. These shared rituals and moral codes build confidence because both parties can predict how the other will act in situations governed by traditional rules.

Trust, however, is something very different. Trust is what is required to establish and maintain social interaction when there is no basis for confidence: when we cannot predict behaviour and outcomes. Trust is what we need when we interact with strangers – who we do not –for whatever reason - consider dangerous. Trust is what is necessary for interaction if the other is unknowable. The other is unknowable when we cannot impute or predict behaviour because either (a) there is no system (formal, legal or otherwise) within which sanctions can be imposed, or (b) there is no underlying sense or terms of familiarity or sameness which would allow such prediction.

Trust emerges at the limits of our knowledge, of our assumed ability to predict behaviour. This idea of limits to our knowledge stands in contrast to the claims made for trust in more locally organized (small scale) societies, often characterized by kinship-based obligations and so with very high levels of prediction, and hence, also, high levels of confidence based on a combination of familiarity and sanctions. Hence to say that societies like Japan and many in Africa where obligations and responsibilities are clearly defined are societies with high levels of trust is, we argue, a misnomer. They are rather societies with high levels of confidence based on well-known and mutually reinforced local, often kinship obligations. Predictability is high, variability low. The system (of obligations, responsibilities, and mutuality) is clear and visible and hence confidence in predictable behaviour is remarkably high.

The corollary to this, by the way, is that whatever is outside the system is totally unknown and hence dangerous. Boundaries are clear and relatively well marked, and when situations arise that do not fit into system categories – such as friendship between individuals in a system that can only "think" in terms of ascriptive, primordial categories – these are translated into terms the system can accommodate: hence the phenomenon of blood-brotherhood, where friendship is symbolically transmuted into a primordial tie. In Rwanda and many other conflicts in post-colonial Africa, it was the opposite which happened– that is, friendships and even conjugal families were dissolved as the more clearly demarked boundaries of blood (e.g., clan commitments and obligations) "trumped" the uncertainty and openness that is the hallmark of friendship.

In all too many cases, (such as among the Dogon farmers and Fulani herders in Mali) communities that had coexisted peacefully for generations became embroiled in violence. As fear and uncertainty spread, many people reverted to ethnic and communal allegiances, leading to violent clashes and a breakdown of the social fabric. Friendships were shattered, and mixed marriages were strained as old ethnic loyalties and survival instincts took precedence over previously shared lives. Similar developments occurred in ex-Yugoslavia in 1992-1995 where 40% of the couples in Sarajevo were intermarried but families nevertheless parted, as religious-based violence overcame even conjugal relations.

In such situations of communal violence, the personal agency of the social actor, which is so necessary to shape interaction into a trustful one, cannot develop. Interpersonal relations become defined in terms of danger demanding appropriate confidence-inspiring measures. This fact then highlights the connection between trust and risk.

Trust is a means of negotiating risk, not danger. In fact, it implies risk (by definition, as a means of negotiating that which is unknown but not all that dangerous). The risk implied is precisely that which is inherent in the freedom of the other – were all action circumscribed only by normative, defined role-expectations there would be no risk, only confidence or lack thereof. Trust, by contrast, implies the risk that is incurred when we cannot "know" the other, and so cannot expect a return or reciprocal action on the alter's part. Thus, as the sociologist Niklas Luhmann claimed, *trust cannot be demanded, only offered and accepted.* Risk, we again note – is not danger! The difference between the two is the difference between situations where trust may or may not be offered.

What is offered (or not as the case may be) is precisely the suspension of judgment and imposition of our own categories on what is different and strange. A willingness to abide with the loss of control, even if it is only the loss of our own internal illusion of control (in the form of presumed ability to categorize alter's acts, motivations, etc.) is in fact the essence of trust; a willingness to abide with that ambiguity inherent to all that is for us, strange and untold. Contra-wise, the imposition of control through the imposition of meaning and judgment is the opposite of trust. For, rather than trust, it is predicated on the need for confidence, on the unwillingness to abide by risk and the uncertainty that everything strange invokes in us.

To remain in a state of suspended judgment, of not knowing (and not claiming to know) the other, is always a risky business, as it demands of us to trust in behaviours that we can neither define nor predict. Agreeing to submit ourselves to this hiatus in explanation, meaning and judgment is no mean feat. It is an extremely difficult and exhausting exercise, for it demands living in suspense, and with an appreciation that our understanding of the situation is incomplete, doubtful, and problematic. We admit a lack of full knowledge, without yet accepting that we live in total ignorance. Indeed, by blurring any absolute distinction between the two states (of knowledge and ignorance) we set up the possibility of thinking through experience, of suspending judgment even as we form new conjectures leading us to new forms of action. We would claim that this is the heart of any experience of living with what is different and unknown. In the particular realm of our interactions with people we understand as different, i.e. as sharing different terms of meaning, participating in different truth-communities, and who generalize trust and a sense of belonging in very different ways, this is especially challenging.

In many parts of Africa, this suspension of judgment—this openness to ambiguity—is difficult, particularly in rural communities that operate within close-knit ethnic or familial systems. In pastoralist communities like the Turkana or the Samburu of Kenya who operate in relatively homogenous social systems, interactions with outsiders are often viewed with suspicion. Confidence is high within the group, but trust is limited when it comes to those outside the community. When a Turkana herder in Kenya, encounters a Kikuyu trader, there is little basis for confidence; instead, trust must be established through shared experience, negotiation, and risk-taking.

This challenge of building trust across ethnic lines has been a central issue in Africa's national politics as well. Politicians often exploit ethnic and clan identities to build a sense of confidence among their supporters, framing other ethnic groups as dangerous or untrustworthy. The creation of these "us versus them" narratives limits the possibility of building a more inclusive and trusting society. During the 2022 elections in Kenya, some politicians sought to instill fear in their constituencies by painting certain communities as threats to their economic or social well-being. In response, many voters retreated into their ethnic enclaves, relying on confidence within their group rather than extending trust to others.

Indeed, in today's world others, that is to say, strangers (members of other communities of belonging), are increasingly experienced more and more as potentially dangerous, requiring the enactment of security measures, and mobilization of law enforcement agencies of different stripes. We frame our interaction with them as requiring confidence-inspiring measures, rather than the mutuality of trust-relations. More and more, fear - that is to say a sense of danger - is the reigning attitude toward those who are different from us. This fear is used increasingly by politicians in many countries, including Kenya, where politicians exploit tribal differences, framing opposing ethnic groups as threats to security and stability. This tactic stirs anxiety, leading to heightened police presence and community tensions, particularly in areas with a history of post-election violence, like Rift Valley. Fear of "the other" becomes a tool for political manipulation, fostering division rather than trust.

How to construct a minimum of trust and the granting of moral credit among strangers remains a huge challenge. How can we come to share some common frame of mutuality with others who remain members of very different communities, tied to different myths, obligated by different commandments, and loyal to different particularities? Can we, in fact, root a shared social life among a diverse populace in something other than the frames of confidence and the presumed knowledge it purports to provide? Have we only abstract and generalized forms of knowledge, as a basis for social life: anything that is, other than the verities of law and the mechanisms of its enforcement?

If confidence, in either positive or negative outcomes of the matter at hand, emerges almost involuntarily from knowledge; trust is an act of will. If confidence is in a strong sense a predicate of our knowledge of an existing state of affairs - or personal traits of alter, or some such - but in all cases of what exists; trust is the creation of new conditions of existence; as stated above, of new potentialities, possibilities, and relations. Confidence reflects existence (or a version thereof), and trust is emergent. It emerges from our capacity to suspend judgment, live in ambiguity, bracket out existing knowledge and tolerate (suffer) challenges to our existing ways of "knowing" the world. We create trust, while we are passive recipients of confidences, based on knowledge usually of a provenance beyond our control.

Sadly, the conditions allowing the development of trust, via shared experience, are rapidly diminishing across many parts of Africa as we share fewer experiences with members of different communities. In several African countries, tribalism and ethnic-based politics have deepened divisions, with leaders increasingly appealing primarily to their ethnic bases. In countries like Nigeria, Côte d'Ivoire, and Ethiopia, ethnic tensions have influenced political alignments, exacerbating social fragmentation. The phenomenon of creating "safe spaces" within universities is also emerging in African countries, as students from different ethnic groups form enclaves, often avoiding interactions with those outside their community. This has extended beyond academic settings into broader social life, where tribal or ethnic affiliations dominate social and political identities for many. Social media platforms like Facebook, WhatsApp, and Twitter, which are widespread across Africa, contribute to this problem by fostering echo chambers where people primarily engage with those who share their political, ethnic, or tribal views.

In Africa's urban centers, we witness increasing segregation of communities along ethnic and economic lines. We have seen places like Kibra slums in Kenya where communities are divided along ethnic lines. This physical and social separation further reduces opportunities for interactions that could foster trust across ethnic and class divides. The rise of vitriolic political rhetoric in Kenya, often fueled by tribal affiliations, is also a major factor. During elections, politicians stoke ethnic fears and tensions, framing elections as a zero-sum game between tribes. This narrative is evident in the political speeches and rallies where communities are warned of "losing" if a rival ethnic group gains power. The 2007-2008 post-election violence in Kenya is a stark reminder of how easily political rhetoric can escalate into violence when trust between communities is lacking. Politicians used social media and community radio stations to spread ethnic hatred, contributing to the clashes between Kikuyu, Luo, and Kalenjin communities.

Attempts to forcefully integrate ethnic communities into pre-existing models, such as the calls for mandatory cultural assimilation or language policies, further limit opportunities for genuine shared experiences. For instance, in some parts of Kenya, there have been efforts to impose one community's language or customs in schools and workplaces, leading to resentment and resistance from other ethnic groups. This approach, rather than encouraging a dialogical process of integration, creates a sense of exclusion and heightens ethnic tensions. The recent trend of anti-immigrant and xenophobic sentiments towards refugees and migrants from neighbouring countries, particularly in areas like Eastleigh, and Nairobi, where Somali immigrants live, has also strained relations. The local population often blames immigrants for economic hardships or security issues, leading to rising tensions. These divisions are reinforced by online narratives that portray immigrants as threats to the local economy or culture.

All these factors severely limit the possibilities of shared experiences and thus the opportunities to develop trust across communal boundaries. Without addressing these issues, Kenya risks deepening its ethnic and political divisions, further eroding the potential for a more integrated and cohesive society.

A not insignificant component of these diverse phenomena in Kenya as elsewhere is precisely their appeals to "knowledge" of some general rule, rather than any willingness to take a risk, i.e., to trust in experience. This unites seemingly opposed phenomena such as tribalism in politics with xenophobia and anti-immigrant sentiments. Both rely on preconceived notions and stereotypes, avoiding any openness to shared experiences.

Tribalism in Kenya often functions on this type of generalized "knowledge." Politicians claim to know the intentions of entire ethnic groups, portraying them as enemies or rivals to their own communities. For example, in some regions, the Kikuyu, Kalenjin, or Luo communities are often painted as aggressors or beneficiaries of state power, depending on who holds the presidency. Similarly, xenophobia directed at Somali refugees in places like Eastleigh or Dadaab is based on assumptions about the criminality or extremist intentions of an entire group. This attitude reflects a general unwillingness to engage with the lived realities of migrants who have fled conflict and seek a better life in Kenya. Just like other forms of prejudice, such as racism or anti-Semitism, which are growing globally, Islamophobia in Kenya mirrors this trend. Somalis, for example, are often viewed suspiciously as potential terrorists, with no need to validate this fear through personal experience or interaction with individuals.

Without trust, there can be no civil society to speak of. However, trust itself rests on some willingness to suspend judgment and a willingness through the sharing of experience to put aside the so-called "verities" of abstract knowledge and rather to *trust* instead to that more embodied knowledge arising out of our shared experience. Our retreat from such shared experience makes the possibilities of a more civil society recede into the background.

The suspension of judgment and so also the risk and attendant discomfort it involves as well as – crucially – the trust mobilized to cope with such a situation, actually serves to validate human freedom, the essential opaqueness of alter's will, e.g. what is most human in her. Simply put: trust recognizes alter's agency, and confidence seeks to limit it. Human agency, free will, and the ontological openness of the human mind: all that gainsay the structures of confidence with its claims to knowledge, are, precisely what makes trust both possible and necessary for the flourishing of communal life.

A sense of shared mutuality thus demands of us to abide by a certain degree of ambiguity and risk and be willing to put ourselves into positions that call for the extension of trust and not continually seek the confidences that our ever-pervasive demands for security seem to provide. So, for example, rather than calls to defend our borders and hunker down behind them, we must realize that our boundaries – that is to say, the boundaries of our own system of confidences - are also the very beginnings of what is new, different, and so challenging and enriching as well. Such a liberating intelligence demands however an act of will and a new political calculus – one which recognizes the value of shared experience rather than an abstract formula for the provision of social trust.

Civility – even individual autonomy – demands nothing less.

Rule #5, All understandings are only partial.

Application: Learn to recognize the terms of confidence when interacting (especially with strangers) and when the leap into trust is necessary.

Group Reflection Prompts:

- Tell a story about a time when you had confidence in a certain situation, plan, or person, but were proved wrong.
- Tell a story about a time when you lacked any basis for confidence and thus were forced into a position of trust. Or, on the other hand, tell a story about a time when you refused to trust.
- Give an example of a time when you trusted a person or group who then let you down.
- Describe the boundary between confidence and trust. Give examples.

Being Uncomfortable

Rule #6 – Uncomfortable is not unsafe.

Living with others is not easy. Living with others who are different from us in important ways is even harder. Sometimes we find difference exciting and enticing. At other times, however, experiencing difference can be discomforting and disorienting. When we encounter those whose religious commitments or moral standards conflict with ours, it often unsettles us. For example, in a rural community in Wajir, a Christian teacher working in a predominantly Muslim community may find it difficult to adjust to the norms of religious observances, such as dressing modestly and observing daily prayer times. These differences can lead to discomfort but they do not automatically signal danger.

Even things seemingly as simple as different culinary or musical tastes can lead to uncomfortable situations in confined urban spaces or relatively isolated rural ones. For instance, imagine a young man from the Rendille community, used to a diet based on camel milk and meat, moving to Nairobi and living with roommates from the Luhya community who primarily eat chicken and ugali. The culinary preferences may be vastly different, causing discomfort initially, but the situation is not dangerous.

Yet still, how should we understand these situations? Do our experiences of personal discomfort indicate the presence of real danger? What happens when we relate to our neighbours as dangerous rather than simply different? What happens when we think that the presence of different people makes us unsafe rather than merely uncomfortable? What kinds of actions might we be willing to justify in the name of safety that would be unconscionable in the name of mere comfort?

The different and the dangerous may evoke similar experiences of personal discomfort, but this does not make them equivalent. The different may simply be that: different. Our discomfort in experiencing difference is understandable. We should not be too harsh on ourselves for experiencing emotional reactions over which we have little control. For instance, in Garissa, a Somali family might feel uncomfortable when a non-Somali neighbour hosts a celebration with loud music late into the night, a practice uncommon in the Somali community. However, we also should not treat our reactions to a situation as an objective assessment of that situation. To immediately conflate our discomfort at encountering difference with the objective presence of danger is a mistake. When we react to the merely different as dangerous, we trigger fight-or-flight procedures that render continued relationships impossible.

After all, feeling uncomfortable has to do with a subjective state arising from a personal experience of unsettledness in relation to a certain situation. As an emotional reaction, discomfort says more about the person or people feeling it than it necessarily does about the external environment itself. Feelings of discomfort, strictly speaking, do not give us any objective information about the source of our discomfort. They only tell us how we feel in relation to that phenomenon. Furthermore, while discomfort may be painful or annoying, we know that feeling uncomfortable does not cause lasting harm on its own. Discomfort, by itself, does not necessarily damage an unfolding relationship.

A sense of danger, on the other hand, is very different. Danger refers to the presence of an active threat of harm in our immediate environment, one to which we must react one way or another. When one is in danger, one is indeed in the presence of the immediate possibility of harm. This harm may be physical, psychological, or both. Either way, in situations of genuine danger, the possibility of lasting harm is an objective and immediate reality. Still, it is important to remember that danger references the possibility of harm, not this possibility's necessary fulfillment.

For instance, during election periods in Kenya, ethnic clashes often erupt, fueled by political manipulation and historical tensions. For a family living in a multi-ethnic neighbourhood, the danger becomes immediate when violence breaks out—homes are burned, people are attacked, and lives are at risk. The physical threat of harm is evident, but the psychological toll is equally profound. The constant fear of violence, the sound of gunshots, and the uncertainty of survival create immense mental stress. Even after the violence subsides, the trauma lingers, affecting trust and mental well-being.

If we hope to live in peace in our different communities, it is going to take a certain amount of social strength. Just as in our own bodies, building this social strength means learning to endure a certain amount of pain. Enduring discomfort can be a growing experience. It exercises our social muscles. Thus, for those who seek to live with difference, distinguishing between the merely uncomfortable and the truly unsafe or dangerous is an essential social skill. Exercising this skill will help build the social muscles necessary to endure the ineradicable moments of discomfort that, from time to time, attend living in human communities. Such exercise begins with distinguishing situations of risk – with their attendant discomfort from those of danger which leave us unsafe.

And indeed, there is an important difference between feeling uncomfortable and being unsafe. While discomfort and danger are often found together, the presence of one does not necessarily indicate the existence of the other. It is possible to feel uncomfortable without being unsafe and to be unsafe without feeling uncomfortable. For example, in Johannesburg, South Africa, a Zimbabwean immigrant may feel uncomfortable while navigating a largely Zulu-speaking neighbourhood, where cultural and language differences can be stark. However, while the situation may evoke feelings of discomfort, there is no actual danger in engaging with local street vendors or asking for directions, as long as the encounter is peaceful.

Despite the logical independence of these two experiences, people are often tempted to interpret their subjective feelings of discomfort as indicating the presence of an objective danger. This interpretation, however, is not always well-founded. When people too readily regard their subjective experience of discomfort as a sign of an objective threat, it becomes almost impossible to maintain productive relationships between different communities. In the case of Johannesburg, if the Zimbabwean migrant mistakenly interprets the cultural differences and unfamiliar surroundings as dangerous, this could limit their willingness to integrate or engage positively with locals.

It is important, therefore, for us to understand both how these two states of being are related and how to discern one from the other in the course of our interactions with those different from ourselves. Distinguishing discomfort from danger allows individuals from various backgrounds to build bridges in multicultural spaces like Johannesburg or Nairobi for instance, where cultural diversity is a defining feature, but misconceptions can easily arise from unfamiliar experiences.

With risk, harm is possible but far from certain. Thus, risk involves the perception of an ambiguous sense of threat. This ambiguity is unsettling. It produces anxiety. However, the uncertainty of risk also leaves room for engagement. This is where the enticement of risk comes in. The unknown element, the potential danger, draws in the thrill-seeker. Risk allows for play. Still, even those of us who are not thrill-seekers often encounter situations of risk, situations of uncertainty. Risk, then, is the type of action we are forced to take when stepping out of our comfort zone, out of the well-known to the unknown. In these situations, situations where we are asked to "take a risk," we are asked to trust. Trust is that which mediates risk. When we trust, therefore, we accept a certain level of risk on faith in something or someone.

Danger references known and immediate threats. Danger, therefore, produces fear. Unlike the ambiguous sense of threat involved in anxiety, fear presents threats that are identifiable and concrete. Presenting itself as a certain thing, danger leaves little to no room for continued or creative relationships. For example, in Mandera, during periods of inter-clan conflict, the possibility of harm is immediate and real, meaning individuals may need to take protective measures. When one encounters danger, eventually, one must fight or flee. One cannot, properly speaking, play with danger. Play requires a type of flexibility that situations framed as dangerous do not allow. Thus, to mediate danger, one must rely on confidence, on systems of security and sanction. Unlike risk, the certainty that attends danger does not allow for the play of trust.

Building a community in a divided world requires taking risks. We must work with others to build peaceful communities, others with whom we may have real differences. For instance, in Nigeria, a country with over 250 ethnic groups, communities from various regions, such as the Hausa, Yoruba, and Igbo, have historically found themselves at odds, especially during periods of political and ethnic tension. Nigeria has seen several ethnic and religious conflicts, including the Nigerian Civil War (Biafran War) and more recent clashes over land, political power, and resource distribution, often framed along ethnic or religious lines.

However, despite this long history of division, there have been notable instances where communities have come together to rebuild relationships and foster peace. One powerful example comes from Jos, in Plateau State, which has seen repeated outbreaks of violence between Christian and Muslim communities, largely aligned with ethnic groups like the Berom and Hausa-Fulani. These conflicts were fueled by competition over land and resources, coupled with political power struggles. Yet, Jos also serves as a place where risk-taking for peace has occurred. In the aftermath of the 2010 clashes, local leaders initiated peace-building dialogues through "Interfaith Mediation Centers," which brought together Christian and Muslim clerics to encourage peace and reconciliation.

These leaders risked a backlash from their groups by fostering inter-community cooperation. They established a dialogue forum where grievances related to historical land claims, religious freedom, and political marginalization were discussed openly. For instance, the Berom and Hausa-Fulani communities agreed to create joint peace committees that would oversee the distribution of disputed land, ensuring that both groups could access resources without triggering further violence. The discussions were tense and required leaders to engage with deeply uncomfortable truths about past incidents of violence. This process involved tremendous risk, as it required both sides to trust that the other would adhere to the agreed terms and not revert to violence.

Women in Jos also played an instrumental role in peace-building. Women's groups from different religious and ethnic backgrounds started economic cooperatives where they pooled resources to support businesses, particularly farming and trade. These women, often survivors of violence themselves, worked together to rebuild the local economy and create platforms where both Muslim and Christian women could share their stories, confront their fears, and find common ground.

Another example of risk-taking in situations of discomfort can be found among the nomadic Fulani herdsmen and the largely Christian farming communities in central Nigeria. These groups have clashed repeatedly over land use and grazing rights, with the herdsmen often accused of encroaching on farmers' lands.

To address this issue, community leaders brokered an agreement where certain lands were designated for seasonal grazing, while others were reserved for farming. This arrangement required both parties to trust that the agreement would be upheld. The farmers had to trust that the herdsmen would not overgraze their land, while the herdsmen had to trust that their cattle would be allowed access to agreed-upon grazing areas. Although fragile, this agreement has helped reduce the frequency of violent clashes in the region.

These initiatives underscore that learning to work with each other's differences is the only viable path toward a world where significant differences between people are no longer a source of conflict. A world without differences is not possible, especially in a diverse country like Nigeria. As long as there are differences, there will be risks, and these risks offer an opportunity for transformation. Nigeria's story shows that the human community is itself a risky business, but it is also one we cannot hope to avoid. By facing the risks and working through the reasonable discomfort that taking risks necessitates, Jos and other regions in Nigeria have managed to move from spaces of ethnic and religious tension to ones of cautious cooperation, with lessons that can be applied across Africa and beyond. As long as there are differences, there will always be risks. Living in a community is a risky business, but it is a necessary endeavour that we cannot hope to avoid.

Considering these truths, we all must learn to distinguish between risk and danger between uncomfortable and unsafe. While uncomfortable may only indicate risk, unsafe may well indicate a real danger. Risk can be mediated and accepted. Risk leaves room for engagement and experimentation. There is an openness to risk. This is not the case with danger. Danger is a close relation. When something is understood as dangerous, we react to it with fear or hostility; neither of which is conducive to the types of ongoing relationships necessary to live with difference.

For those hoping to build community amongst difference, it is necessary to carefully distinguish between situations of danger and situations of risk. Situations of risk, we argue, are unavoidable. Community activists, therefore, should view risky situations as opportunities for building relations of trust. Trust requires creativity and openness, two things found when situations are understood as risky but banished in instances of danger. If, therefore, we too hastily frame risky situations as dangerous, we foreclose creative possibilities for the development and exercise of trust.

Learning to distinguish between those risky situations of unavoidable uncertainty and ambiguity attendant to any existing human community and situations of real concrete danger that threaten to harm the community is a necessary skill for living in a world of difference. While real danger does require systems of security, relying too heavily on such systems destroys the creative openness necessary to build communities of trust. Airport security systems are one thing; increased police patrols and surveillance in Moroccan cities like Casablanca around neighbourhoods with a high population of sub-Saharan African migrants are something else. If one wishes to live at peace amongst differences, one must learn to continually and creatively engage in situations of risk.

Rule #6, Uncomfortable is not unsafe.

Application: Learn to distinguish these two in concrete situations of personal and communal interaction.

Group Reflection Prompts:

- Tell a story about a time when you were so uncomfortable that you felt unsafe. Why do you think this was? Were you really in danger or simply in discomfort?
- Tell a story about a time when enduring a period of discomfort was very important for you. What strategies did you use to make it through this time?
- Tell a story about a time you encountered a difference that made you feel uncomfortable. How did you handle this situation?
- Give an example of a time when mistaking the different for the dangerous might cause harm.
- Which of the two warrants action, and why?

Personal Responsibility and Collective Actions

Rule #7 – Distinguish between shame and guilt.

Membership in a community entails responsibilities. These include not only things that immediately come to mind, like paying taxes or voting but also more complex responsibilities, such as reckoning with the collective actions of the group we belong to—even those that took place before we were born. Being part of a group may not make us guilty for actions we did not personally commit, such as historical atrocities like apartheid in South Africa or colonial-era massacres across African countries, but it does impose a certain responsibility on us due to our ties to the broader community or nation.

These ties often bring with them duties consequent on actions sanctioned by the group. As Hannah Arendt made clear in her essay on "Collective Responsibility": "*There is such a thing as responsibility for things one has not done,*" Arendt explains, "*one can be held liable for them. But there is no such thing as being or feeling guilty for things that happened without oneself actively participating in them.*" She continues: "*Guilt, unlike responsibility, always singles out; it is strictly personal.*" Guilt is something incurred by an individual based on their actions. Guilt, as both a legal status and an emotion ("feeling guilty"), is an individual experience and so very different from the idea of collective responsibility.

Such collective responsibility can be seen in Rwanda, where the entire society engages in *Umuganda,* a national day of service held on the last Saturday of every month. During this day, Rwandans participate in unpaid communal work as an act of national solidarity and collective repentance for the 1994 genocide. This practice is not meant to punish the guilty but to bring people together in a collective act of rebuilding and reckoning with the country's violent past. In essence, Rwandans have embraced a communal sense of responsibility, a responsibility that is not about guilt but about ensuring that the atrocities of the past are never repeated.

With this type of action in mind, we would stress that though they are sometimes used interchangeably in casual speech, responsibility and guilt should not be conflated. Indeed, guilt is one way of parsing responsibility. But there are other ways as well, such as shame. Both guilt and shame are modes of accountability for past actions. But they differ in important ways, and so the obligations assumed by the responsible must be distinguished from the punishments owed to the guilty. Further, responsibility may often be a collective phenomenon while guilt is always an individual one.

Consider the case of post-apartheid South Africa. After apartheid officially ended in 1994, the nation embarked on a process of truth and reconciliation. The *Truth and Reconciliation Commission (TRC)* allowed victims of apartheid-era violence to speak about their experiences while offering a platform for perpetrators to confess their crimes in exchange for amnesty. Importantly, this was a form of collective reckoning. White South Africans, although not all guilty of crimes under apartheid, were nonetheless participants in a system that oppressed the majority black population. Many felt a collective sense of responsibility to atone for this dark chapter in the country's history, even if they were not personally guilty. As a result, efforts to rebuild and reconcile the nation have included collective acts of reparations and economic redress aimed at healing the wounds of apartheid.

Responsibility, when understood as a collective phenomenon, has to do with the liabilities one assumes as a member of a community, a reality to which no person existing within society is immune. Guilt, on the other hand, indexes the debt particular individuals incur when they, in one way or another, harm others. If responsibility is a burden borne upon collective shoulders, guilt is a weight which individuals must carry on their own. At times, responsibility and guilt may tangle together in the complex webs of actual experience. But generally speaking, responsibility and guilt should be understood as referring to distinct processes of accountability, processes often referencing different types of accountable subjects: one collective and one individual. Confusing responsibility and guilt, we argue, hinders our ability to understand and mediate the collective histories to which we are all, in some way, implicated.

The idea of collective responsibility is deeply embedded in many African cultures. The *Ubuntu philosophy*, for example, prevalent in Southern Africa, often summarized as "I am because we are," recognizes that individuals exist within the context of their community. When something goes wrong, such as a family dispute or a crime committed by one person, the entire community often feels a collective responsibility to make amends and restore harmony. This sense of shared responsibility, while not necessarily implying guilt, involves the community in addressing wrongs and maintaining social cohesion. This is especially visible in South Africa's traditional justice system, where community-based solutions to conflicts are prioritized over punitive measures, emphasizing reconciliation and responsibility over guilt.

In Northern Ghana, the Dagomba people use communal labour systems called *N'gorli* to address both collective successes and failures. If a member of the community fails in their responsibilities—whether through personal shortcomings, such as failing to help on a communal farm, or more serious offences like breaking social rules—the community comes together to address it. While the individual may feel guilt for their actions, the entire group shares a sense of responsibility in correcting the failure, ensuring the collective welfare is restored.

Similarly, the idea of collective responsibility is also deeply embedded in the Tanzanian concept of *Ujamaa*, which played a central role in shaping the country's post-colonial identity. *Ujamaa*, meaning "familyhood" in Kiswahili, was introduced by the first president of Tanzania, Julius Nyerere, as a political and social philosophy that emphasized communal living, shared resources, and collective well-being. *Ujamaa* was not just a political ideology but a cultural manifestation of Tanzania's long-standing traditions of mutual support and community responsibility. At its heart is the belief that individuals are interconnected and that a community's well-being is shared by all its members. Nyerere promoted this idea through the village-based cooperative system, where families were encouraged to live together, pooling their labour, resources, and efforts to ensure the collective prosperity of the entire community. When a family faced difficulties, such as a poor harvest, illness, or other challenges, the community would step in to offer assistance, demonstrating the principle of collective responsibility. Similarly, if one member of the community committed a wrong, such as theft or harm to another, the responsibility for addressing the issue often fell to the entire village. This was not about assigning guilt to the community but about ensuring that the wrongdoer was rehabilitated and that harmony within the community was restored. The emphasis in *Ujamaa* was not on punishment but on reconciliation, education, and repairing the social fabric that binds the community together.

Where a sense of collective responsibility presides we will also often find the presence of shame.

To feel shame for one's acts (or even for those of others), one must be tied to others in ways beyond the contractual and in a manner that presumes more than simply material and causal links between our acts and those of others. Shame therefore is a very natural consequence of responsibility for collective as well as self-generated acts. Individually experienced (like guilt) it may nevertheless be rooted in the acts of others to whom we are tied in consequential ways.

During the Rwandan Genocide, many individuals experienced profound shame for acts committed by their communities, even if they did not participate directly. Survivors and bystanders often felt a deep, personal responsibility for the atrocities carried out by people with whom they shared ethnic or communal ties. This collective shame continues to shape reconciliation efforts in Rwanda, as individuals grapple with the moral weight of actions tied to their identity and community.

This brings us to the distinction between shame and guilt. Guilt is personal and is tied to one's direct actions. However, shame can be experienced even for actions committed by others to whom we are connected, such as members of our family, tribe, or nation. In African societies, where familial and communal ties are often strong, shame is a common response to the misdeeds of others. For example, if a respected elder in a Maasai community in Kenya engages in corrupt activities, the entire community may feel a sense of shame, even though they are not guilty of the wrongdoing. This collective feeling of shame can serve as a catalyst for taking responsibility, initiating reparations, and restoring the community's moral standing.

Shame is often tied to collective identity, as we see in the Ashanti people of Ghana, where the community's reputation is paramount. If a member of the tribe is caught in a dishonourable act, such as theft or betrayal, it is not just the individual who suffers the consequences. The entire family or clan may feel the sting of shame and work to atone for the act, often through public apologies or reparative acts. Responsibility, when understood through this lens, is about more than just holding people accountable for their actions. It's about recognizing the interconnectedness of all members within a community and understanding that one person's actions can reflect on the group as a whole. This is evident in African communal life, where the well-being of the individual is inseparable from the well-being of the collective.

Shame differs from guilt however in more ways than one. Guilt, as Herbert Morris has pointed out, is a "threshold" morality: one is either guilty of wrongdoing or one is not. But shame, as he notes, is connected not to a violation but to a failure or a shortcoming. He terms it a "scale" morality, the scale in question being the matrix of our moral identity rather than of any sort of reciprocal relation with another. His passages in *Guilt and Shame* are among the most insightful written on the subject:

> *Shame, unlike guilt, is not essentially tied to fault. Fault is connected with blame and blame is connected with failing to meet demands that others might reasonably place on one because they would place it upon themselves in like situations. Shame, however, may arise through failure to do the extraordinary. We may feel either guilt or shame in behaving as a coward. We may feel shame and not guilt for failing to behave as a hero.*

Shame admits of no simple restitution. Rather, *the steps that are appropriate to relieve shame are becoming a person who is not shameful.* At its extreme we can experience this violation of self as threatening our very existence—the popular phrase, we recall, is "to die of shame," not "to die of guilt." Shame ties identity to sets of expectations of self that are of necessity tied to our community of belonging and our place therein. When as a shoemaker I produce a faulty pair of shoes, I may feel shame at my poor craftsmanship that I later attempt to sell them at an exorbitant price to an unwary customer may lead to guilt.

Shame registers the violation of a sense of self that is posited not in the autonomy of liberal thought, but very much in terms of my community. Shame registers the distance of a self from itself when that self is perceived to exist in relation to the expectations of others, that is, of our community of belonging. It may also register the perceived distance of the community as a whole from its own self-image. The community in question may be as small as a family or as large as a nation.

To the extent that individuals living in so-called modern societies no longer feel part of such communities, they also tend not to feel much shame (except in such family circumstances as noted above). They are left with the feeling of guilt only or perhaps only sometimes, at their wrongdoing. Lacking shame means that they lack pride as well, for one is the concomitant of the other. The cultural images of success—the basketball player spiking a ball, or the successful stock analyst who consummated a deal— reflect not pride but self-satisfaction. There is an important difference. In whom do we feel pride, other than our family members and, more explicitly, our children? We feel pride in their accomplishments as we feel shame at their (moral and other) failings.

These feelings of shame and pride are very much tied to a generalized and collective sense of who we are, quite a part of any notion of individual accountability or guilt. As Arendt notes, the accountability that attends guilt is concentrated and particular; the accountability that attends responsibility, by contrast, is often diffuse and general. Responsibility, Arendt argues, is an unavoidable consequence of the social nature of human existence. Arendt explains it this way: *This vicarious responsibility for things we have not done, this taking upon ourselves the consequences for things we are entirely innocent of, is the price we pay for the fact that we live our lives not by ourselves but among our fellowmen and that the faculty of action, which, after all, is the political faculty par excellence, can be actualized only in one of the many and manifold forms of human community.* To put it differently, responsibility has to do with who one is and to whom one belongs (which parses well with shame), while guilt has to do with what one has done or not done.

As social beings, we are embedded in communities of belonging. In modern, complex societies, we are often members of multiple communities of belonging at once. Some of these communities we enter by virtue of our birth in a certain place at a certain time to a certain family. Others we choose. Some we create. For instance, a person may be born into their ethnic community, such as the Luo in Kenya or the Yoruba in Nigeria, which provides them with a sense of identity, language, and cultural heritage. At the same time, they might choose to belong to other communities, such as a religious congregation like a Pentecostal church or a Sufi brotherhood, which aligns with their spiritual beliefs. Additionally, they may create new communities through shared interests or experiences, such as joining a professional association, a neighbourhood savings group, or a youth-led climate action initiative. These overlapping affiliations illustrate the dynamic interplay of inherited, chosen and created communities in shaping identity and belonging in Africa.

In all cases, we enter realms of collective responsibility by virtue of our membership in such groups. This collective responsibility is part of our social reality and is not something that can simply be escaped by resigning one's communal membership. Even where such resignation is possible, as Arendt reminds us *since no one can live without belonging to some community, this would simply mean exchanging one community for another and hence one kind of responsibility for another.* Thus, the question is not whether we are responsible, but rather to whom and for what are we responsible? An honest and forthright reckoning with this latter question, conducted in good faith, is necessary for living peacefully in societies of difference.

Having said this, we must nevertheless be careful not to confuse responsibility and guilt. As members of communities, we are heirs to the world that those who came before us created. This means we inherit both their accomplishments as well as their atrocities. We are responsible to and for these legacies. However, just as one, as an individual, cannot claim credit for the achievements of those who came before, neither can one be pronounced guilty for the evils done by one's forbearers. The lack of individual participation in evil resolves one of guilt; importantly, it does not absolve one of responsibility and so oft enough of shame as well. As a member of a community, one can be held responsible for the evils of that community's past, even though one is not guilty of them. One's social responsibility may demand that one, as a community member, act to make reparations of some type, one's social membership alone is never sufficient to demand that one be punished for the guilt of another community member, past or present. Arendt explains this dynamic, saying: *In this sense, we are always held responsible for the sins of our fathers as we reap the rewards of their merits; but we are of course not guilty of their misdeeds, either morally or legally, nor can we ascribe their deeds to our own merits.* Maintaining responsibility for a collective past's failures is not the same as being personally guilty of its wrongdoings. For example, the legacy of the slave trade and colonialism continues to spark debates around reparations. Over the last few decades, there have been persistent calls for compensation to address the historical injustices suffered by those subjected to these systems. In Kenya, for instance, British courts ruled in favour of compensating victims of torture under the British colonial regime during the Mau Mau uprising. The compensation, however, was borne by current British taxpayers—individuals who were not personally involved in the atrocities. This case illustrates how societies may collectively bear responsibility for the wrongs of their predecessors without assigning personal guilt to individuals in the present. It underscores the complex interplay between historical accountability and contemporary justice.

Yet, in modern African states, the boundaries between guilt and responsibility can blur and so the question of how to navigate responsibility versus guilt becomes very complicated in cases where atrocities are committed by a group. During the Rwandan genocide, entire communities were implicated in the violence. Many people, out of fear or coercion, participated in the killings. When the genocide ended, the *Gacaca* courts were established as a form of local justice. These courts, rooted in traditional Rwandan conflict resolution practices, aimed to reconcile communities by acknowledging the collective responsibility for the violence, while also distinguishing between those who were guilty of specific crimes and those who were swept up in the broader violence. The focus was not only on punishing the guilty but on finding ways for the community to move forward through collective acts of reparation and reconciliation.

For to be subjected to a claim of responsibility, is not the same as being subjected to an accusation of guilt. Responsibility may demand reparation, as a way perhaps to divest ourselves from the shame of past actions. Guilt on the other hand demands punishment. Confusing these demands destroys any possibilities of reconciliation or justice that may exist. Unfortunately, however, it seems it has become common for those unwilling to engage in the work necessary to live at peace with difference to translate claims of responsibility made against their communities into accusations of guilt. This both misunderstands the nature of the accountability being demanded of their community and confuses requests for reparation with efforts to punish. When claims of responsibility are confused for accusations of guilt, the conversation turns defensive and the messy work of navigating the past in order to create a shared future devolves into misunderstanding and frustration. Misunderstanding and frustration make poor tools for constructing shared futures.

On the other hand, when the guilty seek to diffuse their accountability by translating it into a collective wrong for which they bear only indirect responsibility, justice is ill-served. When looking at the horrendous atrocities of human pasts—whether they be genocides, ethnic or political cleansings, unjust wars, slavery, systematic exploitation of the weak, or any of the other multitudinous programmes humans have concocted to harm one another—it does no good to say that "we are all guilty." This sentiment confuses guilt and responsibility and allows the guilty, those individuals who actively perpetrated harm, to disperse their particular evils throughout the collective in order to escape accountability for their crimes. For, as Arendt notes, *where all are guilty, nobody is.* Punishment is not something that can justly be meted out to a whole collective. Responsibility, however, can be collective. To the atrocities of our collective pasts, we are all, in some way, obliged.

If we seek to live in peace amongst different communities, we must acknowledge that we all have obligations to our communal pasts that may require us to make some form of reparation, to repair broken ties, or to make restitution. Just as post-genocide Rwanda engages in communal acts of reckoning like *Umuganda*, and post-apartheid South Africa continues to grapple with the scars of apartheid through land restitution and reconciliation efforts, many African societies are tasked with confronting their collective pasts. To create a shared future, these societies must distinguish between the guilt of specific individuals and the collective responsibility they all bear for healing the wounds of history.

What exactly needs to be repaired and how exactly this restitution is to be accomplished, however, are complex questions. The answers to these questions will differ from situation to situation, history to history. There is no formula that can be generally applied. Long, hard conversations must attend any good faith consideration of these questions. Thus, here is part of the work of achieving peace between different communities of belonging: working to establish the nature of one's collective responsibility – with whatever shame may attend to shameful actions performed in the past - and working to account for our shared responsibility in whatever way is necessary to create a common future for all members of a society of difference.

Navigating the complex histories of African societies requires a clear understanding of the difference between guilt and responsibility. Guilt pertains to individual actions, while responsibility often involves collective accountability. In African contexts, shame often serves as a social mechanism that drives communities to reckon with their collective pasts, even when no individual guilt is involved. By embracing both the shame and the responsibility for past wrongs, African societies have demonstrated that it is possible to move forward, heal, and rebuild, all while maintaining the delicate balance between individual and collective accountability.

Rule #7, Distinguish between shame and guilt.

Application: Before casting aspersions on a group or individual consider carefully which is the relevant rubric for your ire.

Group Reflection Prompts:

- Tell a story about a time when you were held responsible for something you did not personally do. Why do you think this was? How did it feel?
- Tell a story about a time when you felt guilty about your own actions. Then, tell a story about a time when you felt ashamed about the actions of someone in your community. How would you distinguish these feelings of guilt from feelings of shame?

- What are the societal costs that communities may incur as a result of failure to accept collective responsibility for wrongs committed by the community?
- How do you understand the difference between being held responsible and being punished? Could you give some examples to illustrate the difference between these two phenomena?
- Have you ever desired to leave or switch communities in order to escape responsibility for the community's past? Why or why not?

Knowledge and the Limits of Control

Rule #8 – Knowledge *for* not knowledge *of*.

Living with difference, with others who we do not understand, means living with ambiguity. Living in a community whose ideas, diets, practices, beliefs, calendars, clothes, and other aspects of life differ from your own often leads to situations of uncertainty. Uncertainty and ambiguity are unavoidable aspects of human existence, and they can be quite uncomfortable. When we experience uncertainty or ambiguity, especially those of us raised on presumptions of progress and promises of a wholly tamed world, we often seek to dissipate that ambiguity by seeking out further knowledge.

Knowledge, some proclaim, is the cure for uncertainty. Knowing more, one is promised, can banish the fog of ambiguity, and provide a clear view of the road ahead. Unfortunately, however, these promises and proclamations ring hollow in the arena of actual experience. When it comes to abiding by the inherent ambiguity of living with difference, the question, it turns out, is not about amounts of knowledge; knowing more alone does little. Instead, the crux of the problem turns on the type of knowledge one pursues. The type of knowledge needed for living with difference, we argue, is less the *knowledge of* or *knowledge about* the other, but more the *knowledge for* working together with them.

The phrases *knowledge of* and *knowledge for* represent two distinct epistemological frames. *Knowledge of* searches after essences. It seeks to pin things down, to categorize, to notate, to generalize. It seeks permanence and definitiveness. *Knowledge for*, on the other hand, is much more labile and particular. It is framed in terms of an explicit "to-do". *Knowledge of* is concerned with content. *Knowledge for* is geared toward action. While *knowledge of* asks "what is this?", *knowledge for* asks "what do we need to know in order to do this?" Thus, while *knowledge of* views ambiguity as anathema, an embarrassing lacuna in its explanatory record, *knowledge for* accepts ambiguity as constitutive of any real action taken in a world of contingencies such as ours. In the frame of *knowledge of* ambiguity is dangerous: something to be eliminated.

In the frame of *knowledge for*, ambiguity is risky: something to be negotiated.

For example, many African societies might have their own way of naming and categorizing different ethnic groups and traditions, but this knowledge by itself doesn't foster relationships. *Knowledge for*, on the other hand, is geared toward action. It asks what we need to know in order to work together effectively. While *knowledge of* seeks to eliminate ambiguity, *knowledge for* sees ambiguity as something to be negotiated rather than eliminated.

When it comes to the project of living in communities of difference, ambiguity cannot be wholly eliminated by knowledge. Knowledge simply shifts ambiguity from one area to another. Every answer offered generates even more questions. This is what is behind the assertion, attributed to David Hume, that *explanation is where the mind rests.* A complete, exhaustive, final, once-and-for-all explanation of anything is simply not possible. Our categories of explanation are contingent upon the needs of the moment. And while some moments last longer than others, some may even last centuries, all moments pass. Thus, *knowledge of* the essence of a thing remains inaccessible to us mortals. *Knowledge for,* however, is possible. Unlike *knowledge of, knowledge for* is always defined in relation to a particular shared project; it is what we need to know in order to work together or accomplish some objective. *Knowledge for*, therefore, privileges shared experiences over shared ideas. Focusing on *knowledge for* allows communities of difference to engage in shared projects without first insisting on having shared ideas.

African communities have long understood that complete certainty is elusive. Every answer generates new questions. This is echoed in the proverb: "A wise man never knows all; only a fool knows everything." Our categories and explanations are contingent on the time and situation. Consider the practice of restorative justice in traditional African societies, such as the Gacaca courts in Rwanda, the palaver traditions in West Africa or the *barazas* in Kenya. These justice systems are not based on fixed rules or categories but on the dynamic relationships within the community and the needs of the moment. The goal isn't to categorize individuals as guilty or innocent based on abstract laws, but rather to restore harmony, repair relationships, and create a path forward. This requires knowledge for resolving disputes and negotiating the needs and expectations of all parties involved.

The difference between *knowledge of* and *knowledge for* is connected to their different kinds of goals. The results of inquiries framed in *knowledge of* terms appear in the form of abstract thought. Thus, *knowledge of* is often sought in order to establish certain shared ideas with the other, to find points of convergence in the realm of thought. The realm of thought, however, is a slippery place. Further, as we argue, sharing ideas is not always necessary for engaging in shared projects. Shared ideas seek to build intellectual bonds; shared experience, however, builds bonds based on a common activity, concrete assistance given, and the beginnings of a shared history established. Shared experience may well be a more stable bond than shared ideas. And, luckily, it is easier to begin sharing experiences with those different from you than it is to begin sharing ideas. Thus, *knowledge for* is the type of knowledge that allows one to begin shared projects, it is not necessarily geared toward pursuing shared ideas. In the *knowledge for* frame, shared ideas may come as the result of concrete engagement, but they are not a prerequisite to shared experience.

For instance, when trying to understand a neighbouring ethnic group, *knowledge of* might focus on the group's customs, traditions, and beliefs, reducing them to fixed traits. However, this could lead to stereotyping and oversimplification. We may assume, for instance, that we know all about a particular group because we have been told certain things about them — the way the Akan of Ghana traditionally greet, or the dress code of the Maasai in Kenya. While these insights are useful, they are incomplete. *Knowledge for*, however, asks, "What do we need to understand right now, in this specific interaction, to work together with this group?" It privileges shared experience over shared ideas.

Engagement with the folks around the table is necessary to find out about their own answers. But still, answers to these questions are not directly relevant. Instead, the things one needs to know to pull off this gathering are closer to the following: What kinds of food can everyone at the table eat? What time is best to accommodate everyone's scheduled obligations? Do folks at the table have any accessibility needs that are not being met? Can everyone understand one another, or do we need a translator? *Knowledge of* the deeply held beliefs or practices of each person at the table is not necessarily a prerequisite for engagement. Instead, what is needed is the *knowledge for* putting together a lunch meeting with this particular group of folks. Thus, in this situation, one needs to know about the dietary and accessibility needs of those at the table to ensure that all can participate fully. However, in another situation, different knowledge will be needed, whether it be because there is a different group of people or because there is a different task to be accomplished.

Let's take another scenario, a group of Kikuyu elders, Maasai traditionalists, and urban Nairobi youth planning a community meeting to address land use issues in their area, specifically how to manage grazing rights and agricultural land. They decide to have a joint lunch during this meeting. What kind of knowledge is necessary for this gathering to succeed? In this case, it is not necessary for each group to have extensive prior knowledge about the deep historical reasons behind the Maasai's semi-nomadic lifestyle, why Kikuyu traditions emphasize land ownership and cultivation, or the complexities behind the urban youth's preference for modern, tech-driven solutions to land management. All these topics are fascinating and worthy of exploration in their own right, but they are not prerequisites for these different groups to come together and discuss the issue of grazing and agriculture.

Moreover, assuming that knowledge gained elsewhere about these groups will accurately predict their current perspectives is problematic, as individual members may have varying viewpoints and cultural nuances. Some Maasai may no longer adhere strictly to traditional practices, or some urban youth may have roots in rural areas, complicating any general assumptions. The answers to deeper cultural questions may differ significantly from person to person, and generalizing based on previous knowledge would not suffice. Instead, the knowledge required to hold this meeting focuses on practical issues like: What food can be served that respects everyone's dietary preferences? Should the meat served be halal for Muslims, if they are present? Should it be vegetarian to accommodate those who avoid meat for cultural or personal reasons? What is the best time for this meeting to accommodate the daily responsibilities of the pastoralist Maasai and the working urban youth? Does anyone require translation or interpretation services to bridge language gaps?

While *knowledge of* seeks to understand general content about the other, *knowledge for* seeks out what is needed in order to be able to engage with the other in a specific context on a specific project. *Knowledge for* is always oriented to a particular situation; it seeks not to account for generalities, but for the needs of particular people, at particular times working on particular projects.

It is a fact that as we go about our lives, we cannot do without framing what is new and untold – that is, what is different - into our pre-existing conceptions and categories. We make use of these prior categorizations in all sorts of circumstances, not only with people but when encountering new places, tools, all manner of what philosophers term "natural kinds" (rivers, hills, trees, boulders) as well as more social categories (cousins, clans, siblings, football teams, etc.). We believe that we know and hence respond to the world through our already existing categories which provide the frame by which different 'bits' of information are given meaning primarily through their connection to other 'bits' to form an idea or "a view of the whole". Framing knowledge in terms of *knowledge of,* however, sets up a potentially damaging situation as we mobilize our existing prejudices, preconceptions and "received traditions" to make sense of the situation at hand.

For it is the act of changing, revising, reconfiguring or, indeed discarding our preconceptions—that is of our categories—that causes us discomfort. The armature of our world is shaken, and we must search for a new coherence. It is always much preferred (emotionally) to maintain our existing assumptions, categories, and ways of seeing the world than to admit that they do not adequately encompass experience and so must be revised or jettisoned. We have recently witnessed this very phenomenon during the post-election violence in Kenya in 2007-2008. In some instances, members of different ethnic groups, such as the Kikuyu and Luo, struggled to believe reports from their own family members or friends who had witnessed or been victims of ethnic violence. Many preferred to maintain long-standing beliefs about the peaceful coexistence of their communities or downplay the scale of the conflict, rather than confront the painful reality of political and ethnic tension. This resistance to changing their worldview allowed them to shield themselves from the discomfort of acknowledging the deep divisions that had erupted between once-friendly neighbours.

In many ways it is much easier for us to deny our own experience (or those of our loved ones), or when it contradicts our taken-for-granted assumptions of the world or of the other, to explain it away with some additional bit of information or assumption that leaves our fundamental categories intact. Thus, we will argue the individual "exception" to the rule, rather than challenge the rule's own veracity. Cognitively, it is much easier to claim that this particular Kikuyu, Luo, or Maasai does not conform to our already existing knowledge of Kikuyu, Luo, or Maasai behaviour for any number of contingent individual reasons than to question or perhaps even be forced to revise what we "know" to be the fact about the group in question. For instance, in Kenya, people might assume that a Kikuyu person who is not involved in business is an exception to the belief that all Kikuyu are naturally entrepreneurial, rather than reconsidering the stereotype itself. Similarly, if a Luo individual is seen excelling in a traditionally non-academic field, like farming, it might be dismissed as a personal anomaly, allowing individuals to maintain their preconceived notions about Luo people as predominantly intellectual or politically inclined. This allows the comfort of maintaining a rigid worldview without confronting the diversity within each ethnic group.

In this manner, to maintain our cognitive categories, we re-define our own experience as a particular exception, in order to impose a sort of internal (and imagined) control over the situation, wherein we can shunt the dissonant experience into our existing normative framework without disturbing this framework. In so doing we avoid discomfort. Or perhaps, put better, we trade the more threatening discomfort (of a challenge to our conceptual universe) for the much lesser one of dealing with the exception – making it perhaps the exception that "proves" the rule. In this way too, however, we evade any real confrontation with difference and with the other. We do not accept the challenge that a real engagement with difference implies or the possibilities of learning what may emerge from it.

The default predilection to maintain our existing categories, those that frame given bits of information is a strong one, precisely because the cost in not doing so – in discomfort, if not in cognitive confusion and dissonance – is so great. In some forms of interaction, we may, as indicated above, simply preserve the categories by naming, that is by "categorizing" the particular case that challenges them, as an exception. For it is not any particular bit of information *per se*, that threatens my understanding of the world, of people, groups, and meanings. Rather, it is only when I am forced into a cognitive defence of my whole taken-for-granted world, that is of my existing categories that some form of cognitive "feint" is invoked.

The psychic cost — in discomfort — that we would pay for questioning or revising our categories is generally quite beyond us. The emotional toll involved is not simply that of a cognitive shift of perspectives and with it of some components of our worldview. I In most cases this is challenging enough. But the threat goes beyond these building blocks of our constructed universe. For, by questioning our categories, by doubting or revising our social representations we are also shaking the foundations of our group membership. As social representations are first and foremost social, that is, shared by our in-group; by questioning them we are, inter alia, questioning our group membership, the terms of our collective belonging and so the very foundations of our social selves.

In such circumstances, we are thus thrust into a situation of cognitive dissonance, where a change to our frame of "meta-meanings" is too threatening to our sense of self, while at the same time, our present experience contradicts these very "meta-meanings" which we, willy nilly, bring to every concrete experience.

The result is discomfort. For, how can I continue to be a good Pentecostal Christian in Kenya and also realize that much of what my grandmother taught me about Muslims was actually wrong and based on misconceptions? Growing up, I may have been told that Muslims were violent or that they didn't respect women because of the hijab. These ideas were passed down, shaping how I perceived Islam and its followers. But as I grew older and interacted with Muslim neighbours, classmates, and colleagues, I began to see that these assumptions were inaccurate. Muslim women wear the hijab as a sign of faith and modesty, not oppression, and many of the stereotypes about Muslims as violent were rooted in media bias and not personal experience. What my grandmother taught me was actually wrong and simply based on what Francis Bacon termed so many centuries ago, the "idols of the tribe". To question such "idols", however, necessitates being willing to exist with a certain degree of discomfort, which of course is something we tend to shy away from.

Nevertheless, as a wise psychiatrist from New York City, Theodore Rubin, once said in another context: *The problem is not that there are problems. The problem is expecting otherwise and thinking that having problems is a problem.* And so too with discomfort. Discomfort is only a problem if you expect life to be free of it. Life isn't.

One way to manage the discomfort forged by those contradictions existing between our categories of knowing the other, and our immediate experience of them is through what the American pragmatist philosopher John Dewey termed "suspended judgment". To remain in a state of suspended judgment, of not knowing (and not claiming to know) the other is always a risky business, as it demands of us to refrain from defining and hence predicting other's behaviour, that is precisely to refrain from any claims to *knowledge of.* Agreeing to submit ourselves to this hiatus in explanation, meaning and judgment is no mean feat. It is an extremely difficult and exhausting exercise, for it demands living in suspense, and with an appreciation that our understanding of the situation as incomplete, doubtful, and problematic – and can, at the end of the day, provide us only with *knowledge for.*

While *knowledge of* can be helpful in understanding difference, it is *knowledge for* that allows communities to live and work together successfully. In African societies, where diversity is a reality of everyday life, the ability to collaborate, share experiences, and create shared projects is often more important than intellectual agreement. This practical, action-oriented approach to knowledge helps to bridge differences, allowing people to engage with one another in meaningful, concrete ways. *Knowledge for* embraces ambiguity, focuses on action, and opens the door to shared experiences, which, in turn, can lead to deeper mutual understanding without making it a requirement.

Thus, it is precisely here where we return to the importance of *knowledge for* rather than *knowledge of.* Recognizing the contingent, context and always fungible terms of knowledge, accepting *a priori* that it is severely mediated and can never provide final understanding, but only tools for action is a crucial propaedeutic for the discomfort of suspending judgement as we refrain from any claims to controlling knowledge and seek only the crucial utilities of *knowledge for*.

Rule #8, Knowledge for not knowledge of.

Application: Consider knowledge for (as opposed to knowledge of) as more significant in planning social action with members of other communities.

Group Reflection Prompts:

- Tell a story about a time when you realized you needed more knowledge in order to accomplish a task. How did you go about finding that knowledge? How did the task you were hoping to accomplish shape your search for knowledge?
- How would you describe the difference between knowledge focused on content and knowledge focused on action?
- Tell a story about a time when your general knowledge about a subject was confounded by a particular situation. How does such a story illustrate the structural tensions between general categories and particular circumstances?
- Discuss how the distinction between *knowledge of* and *knowledge for* relates to the distinction between problem-solving and problem-setting discussed at the beginning of the workbook.

Shared Experience versus Shared Meaning

Rule #9 – Allow experience to precede judgment.

On more than one occasion Pope Francis has declared the "globalization of indifference" as one of the greatest challenges facing humanity at the present time. Behind this global indifference is, we would hazard, the ability to isolate ourselves from the sufferings of others and view those people as fundamentally not "the same" as us (whoever "we" may be) and therefore unworthy of our concern. We are endlessly told that, in today's "global village" – with easy travel between distant continents, non-stop news of distant lands streaming into every computer and smart-phone, and near-instantaneous communication across the globe – humanity has been bound ever closer together. It is thus ironic that at precisely this time, global indifference (rather than, say, global solidarity) seems to provide the defining characteristic of our era.

Similarly and on more than one occasion, prominent African leaders and intellectuals, like Desmond Tutu and Nelson Mandela, have declared that one of the greatest challenges facing Africa is the "fractured identity" among its people. Despite decades of pan-Africanism and efforts to forge unity across diverse ethnic groups, languages, States and nations, the reality on the ground often reflects tensions, tribalism, and an ongoing struggle to recognize a shared humanity. Behind this persistent challenge is our tendency to isolate ourselves from the struggles of others, whether they are members of different ethnic groups, religions, or economic classes. We too often see those people as fundamentally "other"—as different from us—and thus, unworthy of our empathy and concern.

In this globalized age, Africa has seen increased connectivity—between cities and villages, nations and regions—through technology, travel, and media. As the "global village" shrinks, one might assume that this would bring us closer together, but ironically, much like in the rest of the world, a "globalization of indifference" has held sway. Despite living in increasingly multicultural environments, where many of us share schools, workplaces, and public spaces with individuals from diverse communities, we still find it challenging to bridge the gaps of communal membership.

The truth is that neither technology nor even physical proximity determines "what counts as the same." Being crowded together with strangers on a packed subway car or *matatu* does not make us neighbours, nor do we share our sense of self with those strangers sitting next to us on a crowded beach. By no stretch of the imagination did either Shylock or Antonio count themselves as "the same" despite sharing the streets of Venice. Walking, talking, buying, and selling together did not produce any consciousness of a shared life in either Jew or Christian. The same of course has been true of slave owner and slave, of colonialist and colonized, of oppressor and oppressed, throughout the ages. "Counting as the same" is, fundamentally, a social act that defines us as a discrete group with our own histories and social categories, ways of understanding, moral judgments, boundaries of what is permissible and prohibited, basic frames of meaning, fears, desires, tastes, smells, and senses of home.

The problem however remains: How can we find a way into solidarity or trust or even empathy, which allows us to be truly different, genuinely diverse? How do we connect with each other without insisting on sameness?

We argue here that openness to shared experience creates the possibility for a new type of empathy across difference, perhaps even of trust to emerge. We may share interaction, without the need to posit sameness. And sharing experience is very different from sharing meanings or a set of beliefs, values, heritages, or even mimetic practices.

Now, it is all too easy to confuse knowledge and experience. And we explicitly mean shared experience, rather than shared knowledge. Experience allows us to assimilate the world quite differently from cognitive knowledge. It is both more practical and more contingent, more powerful, and more specific. It is capable of moving us in new directions as it appeals to our emotions as well as to our intellect. While knowledge can be falsified, experience cannot, although of course the generalizations we make from it certainly can, and often need be. However, when it comes to the problem of empathy and indifference, cognitive knowledge cannot even begin to approach the importance of experience. There is no knowledge comparable to experiencing the *presence* of the other in all her depth, complexity, ambiguity, discomfort, uncertainty, and uncanniness. When we claim knowledge based on the mental assimilation of bits of data, all that we actually have are mere abstractions. Such ideas alone are but weak foundations for any real life, lived with different people.

As in so many other fields, John Dewey is helpful in clarifying this issue. He makes the important distinction between science, as *statements that give* directions or *states meanings*, and art, which *expresses those directions and meanings.* The giving of directions (say to a city) in no way supplies one with an experience of the object of those directions. Statements of direction may be good or bad, confusing, or clear, comprehensive or partial; but in no way can they give us the experience of their object. The map is never the territory. Art, on the other hand, does not simply lead us to an experience; it constitutes one.

This distinction is helpful in the present context. It clarifies the difference between knowledge (of meanings) and the type of playful opening to lived experience that we are advocating. Empathy can only be expressed as an experience. It is constituted in the doing, and only in the doing, in practice. It too is an art. It is the art, if you will, of accepting the emergent rules of interaction that we, with all our differences, define together. We can perhaps compare this to the rules of play, which after all, are not meant to provide meaning, in the sense of notational signification, but only a rough framework of interaction, which is precisely what can emerge from a willingness to hold in suspension our pre-existing forms of knowledge and be open to experience.

Experience, as John Dewey has taught us long ago, is the central component in thinking. *To learn from experience*, he tells us, *is to make a backward and forward connection between what we do to things and what we enjoy and suffer from things in consequence. Under such conditions, doing becomes a trying; an experiment with the world to find out what it is like.* In this process, we cannot separate the intellect from experience, and the attempt to effect this separation actually leaves us with disembodied and abstract knowledge that all too often emphasizes "things" rather than the "relations or connections" between them.

Play defines the "backward and forward" motion (of a ball, person, or whatever is "at play") through which relations are reframed. Very small children do not understand this at first. They will not throw the ball back, for fear of losing it forever. Yet they quickly learn the back-and-forth movement of the ball – its relationships and not just its thing-ness – and in the process begin to establish bonds of trust. A small matter, it would seem, when put thus. Yet it goes to the core of our existence and is on par with what Dewey meant by the painful process of suspending judgment and living in the suspense that results (which is just what play demands). By opening ourselves to experience and so holding judgment in abeyance, we in effect rein in the ego's will to dominate any given situation through explanation and categorization, to put knowledge above experience. We are bracketing out meanings and applying ourselves primarily to the immediacy of the shared experience rather than preexisting interpretive frameworks.

This sharing of experience can, more often than not, challenge our collectively accepted frames or schemes of interpretation – challenge, that is, our systems of shared symbols – of who does and does not, count as the same. Holding such definitions in abeyance – a process that demands the suspension of judgment, the mental pain of such suspension, and the blurring of boundaries – allows a malleability in our approach to our own ideas as well, as critically, to the other. This is in essence a form of play, which permits us, at the best of times, to think through our existing relations with other people in a way that would not be possible if predicated solely on either shared memory or an enacted mimetic practice. New conjectures, new judgments, and a new experience of thinking are now possible, as the experience of difference is disentangled from existing judgments, conjectures, and received meanings.

Indeed, we have all felt the power of a shared experience – in schools, summer camps, the military, our university years or even a long tenure in a job which required close work with colleagues. Moreover, such shared experience, when paired with collective reflection upon that experience, often creates a sense of belonging. When managed well, shared experience congeals an aggregate of individuals into a group. Shared experience can establish a sense of communal belonging even when shared meanings are elusive. Shared meanings, common understandings, and agreement are often presupposed as principal elements of any community. But as anyone who has lived in any existing human community knows, the extent of agreement and shared meaning in any group is often quite limited. Communities may be sufficiently bound together by shared practices even when they disagree on the ultimate meaning of those practices.

As a basis for community, shared meaning relies on beliefs, doctrines, creeds, or other abstract ideas to bind people together. Shared meaning rests largely on people thinking and feeling the same as a source of connection. Thus, shared meaning aims to standardize interpretations and finalize explanations across the entire group. Shared meaning, as a communal aim, works toward ideological purity, doctrinal orthodoxy, or right beliefs.

Shared experience, however, has more limited aims. Shared experience relies more on spending time together and completing shared projects as a way of building connections. Shared experience, therefore, eschews standardization and finality in favour of particular and concrete engagement. Shared experience deals far more with the concrete than the abstract. If shared meaning operates in the realm of ideas, shared experience takes place in the realm of actions.

In the African context, shared meaning often arises within communities that are bound by deeply held cultural traditions, religious beliefs, and practices passed down through generations. For example, in many African societies, rites of passage serve as a powerful example of shared meaning. Among the Kikuyu of Kenya, the circumcision ceremony, or *Irua*, is not just a physical act but is loaded with symbolic meaning for the entire community. This ceremony marks the transition from childhood to adulthood and is tied to ideas of responsibility, identity, and community belonging. It connects individuals to their ancestors, aligns them with their clan's history, and cements their place within the larger cultural group. The shared meaning here is derived from a common understanding of what it means to be Kikuyu, to undergo *Irua*, and to uphold certain values.

Contrast however shared meaning to shared experience which operates according to different metrics of time. If shared meaning -as in the above example - seeks to speak in terms of "all time," shared experience speaks only about "this time." Shared meaning seeks agreement and consensus. While these are desirable ends, agreement and consensus are difficult to establish and maintain, especially amongst a group of people who differ from one another in important ways. Shared experience, however, is more modest; it seeks only engagement. On the basis of this engagement, in the process of doing things together, we maintain, that a sense of belonging can develop, even amongst those who do not share much in the realm of meaning.

Shared experience occurs when a group of particular people in a particular circumstance in a particular location do something together. Regardless of the event, shared experience requires proximity and concurrence. People have to be together to have a shared experience. Shared meaning does not require this same spatial and temporal relationship. Shared meaning operates in the realm of generalities and abstractions freed from concrete time and place. It is precisely for this reason that wholly shared meaning is so elusive. Further, while shared meaning seeks to collapse a whole field of possibilities into a single path on which all members of the community must walk, shared experience is much more open, especially to those of different communities. Shared experience, we believe, can build and maintain a sense of belonging while leaving open possibilities for disagreement, divergence, and importantly, for difference.

Yet simply being together at an event is not enough to fully share an experience. There is a difference between a concurrent experience and a shared experience. Multiple people may be present for the same event at the same time, but that does not mean that they have a common experience. In fact, many different people may experience the same event in significantly different ways. Consider the example of a Christian missionary attending a traditional African religious ceremony, such as a Yoruba *Bàtá* drum performance, which is used in rituals to communicate with the Orisha, particularly during the worship of *Sango*, the god of thunder. For the Christian missionary, this experience might be viewed skeptically or perhaps with discomfort due to their monotheistic beliefs and rejection of what they perceive as polytheistic practices. Their understanding of the ceremony is shaped by their Christian teachings, their cultural background, and perhaps even preconceived notions about African traditional religions. How different is it then from a devout follower of the Yoruba faith participating in the same event, which evokes deep emotional, spiritual, and cultural responses that are tied to their ancestors and the spiritual cosmos they believe in? This then would be a concurrent experience that still needs the element of what we are calling reflective practice to turn it into a shared one.

Reflective practice is the means by which a concurrent experience becomes a shared experience. Reflective practice happens when a group of people all experience the same event and then set aside time later to sit together and process that event collectively as a group. This act of collective processing, of talking through each person's individual experience in the context of the group, allows a space for the differences within their experiences to emerge. These group conversations after an event, more often than not, reveal that, even though the whole group was in the same place at the same time, people in the group had very different perceptions, understandings, feelings, and thoughts about what was happening. Talking through these differences of experience allows room for the group to come to a collective understanding of how the group, as a whole made up of many different parts, experienced the event. Through reflective practice, the group can create a collective story to tell about the event. They may not all agree on the meaning, purpose, or outcome of the story, but in the act of reflecting together on an experience, the disparate experiences of each individual congeal into the shared experience of the group.

When ideological congruence, total agreement, or doctrinal purity are made prerequisites to engagement, then shared experience with those who are different from us becomes impossible. Furthermore, when shared experience is viewed as a mere pathway intended to lead to shared meaning, one will be constantly frustrated. Such a path rarely terminates in a single location. It twists and turns, frays and splinters. Wholly shared meaning is slippery, it slides through one's fingers as soon it's grasped. Treating shared meaning as a necessary condition of community renders living with difference impossible. Shared meaning demands sameness. It leaves little room for difference. Shared experience, on the other hand, demands only participation. Participation can be undertaken by a whole host of different peoples. Thus, shared experience moves the necessary "sameness" of community-building from the abstract realm of ideology and doctrine into the concrete realm of practice and participation.

Furthermore, shared experience, grounded as it is in the particular, concrete circumstances of any given moment, allows room for negotiation. In most cases, one need not give up their convictions, violate their beliefs, or neglect their obligations in order to share experiences with others. When it is made clear that engagement does not necessarily imply agreement, people are able to share experiences with one another while preserving their own sense of self. These types of interactions involve boundary play. Shared experiences allow us to play on the margins of each other's communities which, in turn, enables new forms of community to be constructed without dissolving our connections to other communities of belonging. Of course, boundary play has its limits. Things only bend so far before they break.

In order to share experiences across communities of belonging, accommodation and attention to those non-negotiable aspects of our various selves is necessary. Not all experiences can be shared with all people, but all people can share some experiences. It is in the second half of this axiom that we must place our hope. That, we pray, is enough.

If empathy and living with difference are to be a permanent and integral aspect of our relations with others, they must emanate from experience and practice rather than a particular ideological position or a priori interpretive framework of what "counts as the same". In other words, they must be born of experience rather than ideology. This suspension of our existing notions of "what counts as the same" is, I claim, the key to any further progress along the path of concern for the other, a concern that must always be concrete and experiential. And hence our rule:

Rule #9, Allow experience to precede judgment.

Application: Strive to maximize shared experience over prior judgements when interacting with strangers.

Group Reflection Prompts:

- How would you explain the difference between a parallel experience, one that happens at the same time but separately, and a shared experience?
- Tell a story about a time when your reaction to an event was different from that of your peers. Why do you think different people had different reactions to the same event?

- Give an example of an experience you could share with others without sharing meanings. Explain why this experience does not need shared meanings.
- Give an example of an experience that you could only share with people who share your meanings. Explain why having a shared understanding or shared meaning is important in this situation.

Negotiable vs. Non-negotiable

Rule #10 What we hold to be sacred is also non-negotiable.

Since the earliest of times, people have exchanged multiple and different sorts of items: goods, services, ideas, and even people (marriage has often been seen as an exchange of women – and sometimes men - across kinship groups, not to mention the taking and capture of slaves). This exchange took two primary forms. One was in the form of a gift and the other progressed through some process of negotiation (and conflict and conquest are also a form of negotiation).

Among the Yoruba of Nigeria, as in many communities across Africa, marriage has long been seen as a form of exchange between families. The groom's family presents the bride's family with a bride price, a culturally symbolic gift that signifies respect and appreciation. This bride price is not a simple transaction of goods, but a complex social exchange that solidifies relationships between two kinship groups. Negotiations over this price are both delicate and necessary, with different items such as yam, kola nuts, or goats sometimes included, depending on the families' agreement. Such exchanges have deep social and cultural meanings, cementing the bonds between families while respecting each other's traditions.

Even in more informal settings, such as the markets of West Africa, negotiation is a key component of everyday exchanges. The market in Accra, Ghana, is a social space where bargaining over the price of a piece of kente cloth or handmade sandals is expected. The buyer and seller engage in a dance of offers and counteroffers, rooted in both respect and economic need. The final price is not just about the value of the item but also about building rapport and establishing ongoing relationships. For both parties, it's not just a transaction but an exchange of social capital and trust.

We have always exchanged with one another and always, when not done through wars and conquest, we have done so through some process of negotiation (wars too can be seen as a type of negotiation, albeit of a particularly violent nature). We exchange so much labour for so much money; or earlier, so many bushels of barley for so many barrels of apples and so on. Our negotiations are themselves influenced by many factors. Economists tend to stress supply and demand curves; psychologists and social psychologists stress group dynamics and negotiation skills and political theorists tend to point out various external restrictions on the negotiating process.

After all, not all markets (exchange forums) are open to everyone (a plumber cannot legally negotiate to perform open heart surgery) and almost all markets are structured in various ways. Minimum wage laws, overtime, and child labour laws, among other restrictions, limit what can and cannot be negotiated. (An employer cannot offer less than minimum wage, cannot hire a minor, and must respect shift hours or pay overtime). Of course, people seek many ways around these limitations, such as calling uber drivers self-employed contractors rather than employees for example, and often the laws are honoured in their breach more than in compliance. But the laws do exist and those involved in the exchange are accountable to them.

Different societies have different restrictions on negotiation. In medieval Christendom, the taking of interest on loans was prohibited. In the Islamic Kingdom of Andalus, it was illegal to build a church higher than a mosque. All these are, of course, restrictions on exchange (even if the Christian community desires and can afford such a high Church and the architect can plan it, it cannot be built. Or, in the second case, both lender and borrower agree on terms of interest, but the transaction still cannot be legally concluded in those terms). Minimum wage, child labor laws and overtime are of course 20th century innovations. The nature of such restrictions can thus also change over time in the same society. This change moreover is itself a process of negotiation, sometimes violent, as the history of union movements in many countries makes clear. Minimum wage, child labour laws, overtime, and many other restrictions on contract – on what could be negotiated – were the result of bitter struggles over many decades. They should not be seen as some self-evident, always-existing state of affairs. They were arrived at via conflict – which as we said earlier is, itself, a form of negotiation.

Different societies, as just noted, have always imposed their own restrictions on what can be negotiated or exchanged, and African cultures are no exception. Both lender and borrower may agree on terms of interest, but the transaction may still not be legally valid if the agreement runs afoul of the law. For example, in pre-colonial Buganda (in modern-day Uganda), the Kabaka (king) held ultimate authority over land distribution. The land was considered the property of the king, and subjects could not legally negotiate its sale or ownership without his approval. Chiefs were granted land by the Kabaka in return for loyalty and military service, but they could not trade or sell this land freely. The power to allocate land was both a political and economic tool, used to reinforce the hierarchy and ensure loyalty to the monarchy.

In the same way, in many African kingdoms and communities, certain resources or practices were bound by sacred rules. Among the Shona of Zimbabwe, the land was also deeply tied to ancestral spirits. Negotiating the use of land for farming or hunting had to follow cultural protocols involving ancestral approval. Before land could be farmed, rituals were performed to ask for the ancestors' blessings, and if these rituals were not performed, it was believed that the harvest would fail or that other misfortunes would follow. The restrictions on land use and ownership were embedded in spiritual and cultural laws, beyond mere economic agreements.

However, it is crucial to recognize that not everything is negotiable. In the same manner, not everything can be given as a gift. We know this from our own lives and experiences as well as from the work of scholars studying and writing on gift-giving in different cultures. Beyond gift-giving, however, is the more important point that not everything is negotiable. Our discussion above on the limits to exchange pointed precisely to certain arenas in which there could be no negotiation – at least in the legal sense of the term. In many African societies, there are sacred, non-negotiable aspects of life and community that mirror the limits to exchange seen elsewhere in the world. For example, the Luyha people hold the land on which their ancestors are buried as sacred. Land can not be sold or traded away to outsiders because it is not just a commodity but a part of their spiritual heritage, where the ancestors reside. Attempts to purchase or negotiate for such land would be seen as deeply offensive and unacceptable. This is still the case in many African communities today, where land is held collectively, and the idea of individual land ownership for sale is at odds with their traditional values.

Other items or forms of labour may also be non-negotiable; and not open to a back-and- forth of mutual bargaining, wheeling, and dealing and general deliberations. There are non-negotiable cultural and spiritual practices that guide behaviour, especially in the context of hospitality. For instance, in many communities in East Africa, such as among the Kikuyu or Luo people of Kenya, hosting guests involves certain rituals and expectations, but some things remain off-limits.

Consider a coastal town in East Africa, where a Swahili Muslim guest is invited to a feast by a family from a different ethnic group, perhaps from a largely non-Muslim community. In this coastal region, where Islamic customs are deeply rooted, certain dietary laws are strictly observed. The host, eager to show hospitality and share their best food, prepares a grand meal, which includes a roasted pig—a delicacy in their culture and a symbol of celebration. The Swahili guest, however, being a devout Muslim, will not consume pork. Even though the host has gone to great lengths to prepare the meal, the guest will kindly refuse to eat the pork, explaining that it goes against their religious beliefs. The host, in this case, might feel disappointed or even embarrassed, but the refusal is not negotiable for the Muslim guest. While the guest may partake in other dishes, like rice or vegetables, they do not particularly like in order not to offend their host (in a sort of internal negotiation of what they can and cannot abide), the consumption of pork is simply impossible, regardless of the context.

We all, both individually and as part of different collectivities (nations, clans, religious communities and so on) have multiple items or actions which are non-negotiable, regardless of the consequences to us or to others. In many ways, these represent what we hold most sacred. The sacred is non-negotiable. And, for better or worse, we hold different things sacred. Your totem is my lunch. And my wonderful high-priced champagne is for you an abomination.

And here is where the problems begin. In the Luyha community, it is customary to perform several rituals when preparing the deceased for burial. One such practice is laying a *sanda* (a type of shroud or burial cloth) on the body of the deceased before they are buried. This ritual is deeply rooted in the belief that the dead should be sent off with dignity and respect, and the *sanda* represents the community's final gift to the departed, ensuring they are covered and protected in the afterlife.

Now imagine a scenario where a member of the Luyha community passes away, and their family gathers for the funeral. However, one of the deceased's children recently converted to a Pentecostal denomination that views such traditional rituals as unbiblical. This child refuses to participate in the laying of the *sanda*, believing that such a practice contradicts their Christian faith, which teaches that the soul does not require such material coverings in the afterlife. The rest of the family, particularly the elders, will be deeply offended by this refusal. To them, laying the *sanda* is not just a cultural tradition; it is a non-negotiable aspect of honouring their dead and fulfilling their duty to their ancestors. They cannot comprehend why their kin would reject such an important ritual. And the child too is constrained by his sacred beliefs which are in direct contradiction to those of the rest of the family and community.

Similar situations happen throughout the world and are not easily negotiated. Why would a devout Muslim refuse to drink the local brew at a rural gathering, even though everyone was passing around cups of it, brewed by the grandmothers? This refusal would offend the elders, who see it as a rejection of the community and its traditions. Shouldn't we all have been more accommodating of the collective expectations, setting aside these small cultural and religious differences for the sake of unity? There is no optimal "solution" to these challenges, other than to negotiate them with a sense of humility and modesty.

On the other side, we must all be mindful not to turn every preference we may have into a non-negotiable principle. It is an easy and dangerous move to make. Something may even be very important to me, precious and value-laden but that in itself does not make it non-negotiable. In certain circumstances and with certain stakes I may be willing to forgo it. If so, it is not for me non-negotiable, and I should not present it as such – not to myself and not to others. When I do so I am inconveniencing others simply to gain a benefit, not to prevent what for me would be a sacrilege.

Such situations notwithstanding, the problem of sacrilege is really the heart of the matter. What we hold sacred is not the same across countries and cultures. The Maasai, for example, practice bloodletting in their cultural rites, which involves pricking a blood vessel in a cow's neck to drink its blood while keeping the animal alive. For the Maasai, this is a sacred act deeply tied to their identity and way of life, whereas for animal rights groups, it would be seen as an abomination and a violation of animal welfare.

A similarly divisive issue is female genital mutilation (FGM), which is still practiced in parts of Africa as a rite of passage for young girls in certain communities. For many human rights activists, FGM is seen as a violation of bodily autonomy and children's rights, an unnecessary and harmful procedure. For some of the communities that practice it, however, it is viewed as a critical cultural ritual and a marker of transition into womanhood that is non-negotiable and sacred.

These then are examples of an un-reconcilable clash of non-negotiable positions- each informed by very different ideas of community, self-hood and of the sacred. There is moreover, and as noted above, no algorithm for their solution. The most that can be hoped for is that through mutual goodwill, a bracketing-out process can be affected that will let the parties to any dispute of this nature find a temporary, contingent and case-specific "solution" to the particular matter in contention, without having to refer to the sacred and non-negotiable principles on which their different positions rest.

Rule #10, What we hold to be sacred is usually non-negotiable.

Application: Learn to distinguish your own (and others') negotiable from non-negotiable positions.

Group Reflection Prompts:

- Give an example of what, for you, would be non-negotiable. Explain why.
- Can you think of something which you thought was non-negotiable for you and, over time or when faced with a decision, you realized that it was not?

- On the other hand, can you think of a situation where, before the fact, you thought compromise and negotiation were possible but when actually faced with the reality, realized that you could not make any compromises in your position without compromising who you are?
- How would you find a solution to a clash of non-negotiable positions?

Saving the Commons

Rule #11 – There is no monopoly of suffering

Sometimes benign, but increasingly less so, the claims of a community challenge the liberal order of individual rights in untold ways and with as yet unknown consequences. The challenge is – as noted earlier - how to accommodate these claims without necessarily accepting the demands that, more often than not, go with them. How can we articulate a politics of belonging—which we recall, always embraces some exclusionary element—without succumbing to the rhetoric of the extreme right both at home and abroad? While continued advocacy of individual rights may well be necessary, rights by themselves are a far-from-sufficient condition for human flourishing and satisfying the need for roots; a sense of belonging must be accommodated if we are to be spared a replay of some of the worst horrors of the last century (such as the perpetrated under the Soviet, Nazi and other totalitarian regimes).

Since time immemorial, all societies, including those across the African continent have experienced struggles that reflect both communal challenges and personal hardships. These struggles often stem from claims of community, where group identity and tribal affiliation can challenge the modern ideals of individual rights. In places like Kenya, we have seen conflicts between pastoralist and farming communities over grazing lands and water sources. These cause cycles of violence, exclusion, and resentment. The question is how to accommodate these deep-rooted communal identities without succumbing to the exclusionary and sometimes extreme demands that come with them.

How can we create a politics of belonging—always recognizing that belonging includes some exclusion—without falling into the rhetoric of divisiveness, which we have seen cause havoc in different African societies, from South Sudan to South Africa? The advocacy for individual rights remains important, but rights alone are not enough for human flourishing. We must recognize the African context where the sense of community, connection to the land, and a shared history are as important as personal freedoms. Our challenge is to blend both individual rights and a deep sense of community if we are to prevent repeating the horrors of Rwanda's genocide, or the prolonged ethnic conflicts in places like Côte d'Ivoire.

While there are no easy solutions to our current situation, there are a number of steps we can take to meet this challenge. Eschewing both the hard and impenetrable boundaries being set up by nationalist politicians between "us" and any manner of "them", as well as the ultimately homogenizing politics of abstract human rights that makes every individual a morally autonomous agent devoid of inherited ties and obligations, a rigorous engagement with communal differences is called for and the way we do so is all important.

To begin, we must always remember that knowledge, that is to say, morally significant knowledge is always collective, not individual. What we know, we know collectively, as part of a group. Our categories, ways of understanding, moral judgments, boundaries of what is permissible and prohibited, basic frames of meanings, fears and desires—all of these are, in a strong sense, social. We hold them together with others, and not simply as individual beliefs.

As knowledge is collective, we must understand that knowledge is bound up with whom we trust. Almost always, we are called upon to grant moral credit to some source in matters that are, by their nature, almost always morally and often factually ambiguous. In such circumstances, the set of relevant external bits of information and histories needed to explain them will frequently be decided on the basis of our group belonging and the moral credit that we, as members of one or another group, grant to the act of inclusion or exclusion of information. Doing so determines what is relevant or irrelevant to interpreting any particular case.

For instance, in the Great Lakes region of East Africa, trust within ethnic groups such as the Hutu or Tutsi dictates whose interpretation of historical grievances and reparations we believe. Similarly, in the Somali community, clan-based decision-making remains a central feature of life. Trust in the clan elders (known as *Guurti*) and the moral credit granted to them often determines what is considered legitimate or true, particularly in conflict resolution, land disputes, and even in matters of marriage and social relationships. The *xeer* system of customary law rather than that of written contracts or modern courts determines how conflicts over land and water rights are resolved in a system built on trust, loyalty, and shared historical - even mythical - experiences.

Communities are real-life active entities within which human actors are born, thrive, live, die, and make sense (or don't) of their worlds and the worlds of others. We cannot live without these communities and, despite all the dangers that may arise from them, there is no possibility of human life or achievement outside them. Consequently, as we strive to share a common life with others, it is important not only to stress what we may have in common with the other, what is therefore generalizable but also to accept and attempt to build on our differences - what is invariably particular. For our differences are precisely the markers of different communities of belonging that define who we are and that provide the settings in which we live our lives and where we feel most secure.

Our goal should be to see just how far we can build trust and, hence, a common store of knowledge across different communities. Can we construct some minimum—a "good enough"—framework of trust, in some very small arenas of knowledge and interaction, that will in turn allow us to construct a shared frame of reference that will permit us to act in concert and perhaps even be drawn upon when events that may divide our different communities threaten the ability of our fellows to live their differences together? To what extent can we grant moral credit (trust) to others--to those who are not members of our own group—and so share with them some common frame of understanding and knowledge, despite being members of very different communities, tied to different myths, obliged by different commandments and loyal to different particularities?

To do so we must seek to construct a set of experiences that are shared but that also leaves room for the particular, the concrete and the unique. By sharing experiences, we can perhaps find a way to build trust, even as we remain loyal to our own particular communities of trust and belonging. The shared experience of what can be called "embodied knowledge" is central to any attempt to construct new frames of understanding across different communities of belonging (or at least to point at that possibility). Shared experience provides the necessary basis for constructing what are, by definition, new frames of knowledge across our different communities of belonging—providing the needed balance of generalized and particularized pedagogies.

When my experience of the Jewish other or the Moslem other or the Sikh other, in all their varieties and differences and subtle particularities, begins to compete with my taken-for-granted understanding of what is a "Jew" or "Moslem" or "Sikh"; when I see what I can share with him or her, and what I cannot; and when my worst enemy turns out not to be the devil incarnate, not some bogey-man with horns, but simply a member of an ethnonational group, involved in a horrific struggle over land with another ethnonational group to which I may feel particular ties of attachment (though I live thousands of miles away)—then I have begun the process of what can be called turning knowledge *of* into knowledge *for*. Here, we approach what should be a core principle: shared practice, rather than simply shared ideas or meanings, must be focused on knowledge *for* rather than knowledge *of*. Conditional knowledge, which is knowledge that has been framed for a specific purpose, can be shared across communities—even as our categorical propositions, our "assertive" knowledge, remain firmly rooted within our different communities of belonging.

Two objectives, then, are achieved through shared experience and embodied knowledge: the first, widening somewhat the circle of trust, those to whom we may grant moral credit, to those who may not be members of our own community of belonging—but with whom we have perhaps mingled our labour. The second is the reframing of the knowledge that is necessary to such shared work and so also a shared world with the other—from knowledge *of*, to knowledge *for*—from those propositions which we categorically assert, to those which embody conditional knowledge relevant to some shared purpose. Both, hopefully, bring us to a point where experience precedes judgment—individualized experience balancing our always generalized taken-for-granted assumptions—rather than, what usually happens, the other way around.

In many ways, the emphasis on experience preceding judgment brings to mind the writings of the father of American pragmatist philosophy, John Dewey. Deweytaught us to pay greater heed to experience, rather than to our always-already-existing perceptions. In fact, Dewey attempted to teach us to think in new ways--to think, as he termed it, "reflectively." Yet, he cautioned, *Reflective thinking is always more or less troublesome because it involves overcoming the inertia that inclines one to accept suggestions at their face value; it involves the willingness to endure a condition of mental unrest and disturbance. Reflective thinking, in short, means judgment suspended during further inquiry; and suspense is likely to be somewhat painful. . . . To maintain a state of doubt and to carry on a systematic and protracted inquiry—these are the essentials of thinking.*" Thinking through, considering, experiencing, and suspending judgment even as one forms new conjectures, can lead us, hopefully, to new forms of action.

Our encounter with the other has the potential to open up new possibilities for understanding, self-reflection, and, ultimately, action. To realize this potential, however, we must be willing to meet the other as an equal, outside of institutional, national, and international hierarchies. We must be open to the other and to the dialogue that may ensue. Such a dialogue implies, as well, our willingness to relinquish control of the developing encounter. While not negating ourselves, we must nevertheless abandon our inherent desire to control the situation and order it according to our own dictates. This is not easily achieved. But it is not impossible either. Unfortunately, however, it seems to be something members of "the international community", development NGOs and such, find very difficult to do.

It is said that an explanation is that place "where the mind rests," meaning that once an explanation is given, the examination of further (additional or alternative) explanation stops. And what a genuine dialogue entails, of course, is, precisely, a willingness to change the place where the mind rests. Now minds are very busy things—constantly moving, restless, questioning and querying. When then does the mind rest? Most often, it rests when the particular purpose of its questioning has been fulfilled and all too often this is in a confirmation of our already existing assumptions, conjectures, and prejudices.

In terms of the construction of a shared social world, we must therefore learn to be open to experience—rather than preconceived ideas and abstract forms of knowledge. We must enter a process that can only be realized through a slow, cumulative, mutual and not always conscious process of straddling the boundaries of our existing and developing modes of thought through the challenges of shared action, that is, through embodied experience.

For the experience of the other, the encounter with the other—can only be expressed in action. It is constituted in the doing, and only in the doing—in the practice, in the pragmatic orientations taken when we find ourselves in the midst of an uncontrolled encounter with what is different, in the midst of acting together. Experience is much more art than science. In fact, I would say that the art of the encounter with the other, and the openness to the transformative potential this encounter contains, actually constitutes experience.

It is in this context no surprise that in his classic study on *The Nature of Prejudice* in 1954, Gordon Allport specified that simple inter-group contact was not enough to dispel prejudice between social groups (an incorrect assumption of many contemporary practitioners of "contact theory"). Allport in fact specified that *Only the type of contact that leads people to do* [emphasis in original] *things together is likely to result in changed attitudes. ... It is the cooperative striving for the goal that engenders solidarity.*

He goes on to explain the strong positive correlation between shared work on joint projects and the diminution of prejudice. Association predicated on both equality of status and a joint "doing" are the perquisites not only for the emergence of a new sense of solidarity but also for the lessening of prejudice. They are, similarly, the preconditions for the emergence of new understandings, new frames of knowledge and so the revision of our always already existing categories and taken-for-granted assumptions. The endless phronetic recalibration of knowledge is an aspect of every craft: from electrician to roofer to fiction writer and surgeon. There is no reason why it should not play a similar role in all situations of "intercultural communication" as well.

All communities, regardless of their history, bear some form of suffering. Whether it is the Kikuyu in Kenya, the Fulani in West Africa, or the Shona in Zimbabwe, no community holds a monopoly on historical or present-day grievances. Thus, engaging with others through shared experiences and embodied knowledge—acknowledging differences without falling into divisive rhetoric—will ultimately allow us to construct a shared future, one that honours both individual rights and the deep sense of community that is central to African life.

Applications of Rule #11:

We would like to end by presenting the following as a "tool-kit" of possible ways to engage fruitfully in a shared common life – summarizing much of what has been discussed throughout this sort of treatise.

Hold all claims to absolute truth in abeyance. In terms of concrete action, most such claims are irrelevant and often counterproductive. (Just as one does not need to know reigning theories of subatomic particles in order to cut the wood for a living room shelf, a Maasai or Luyha doesn't need to understand the complexities of Kalenjin initiation rituals in order to cooperate on building a new school.

Recognize the partial nature of any and all understandings. "Explanation is where the mind rests"; it is never the place of full knowledge, but only of a purpose well-served.

Allow experience to precede judgment. Bring in the minimum assumptions needed to get the job done, rather than a checklist of principles against which the experience itself is to be verified.

Enacting the above involves a certain degree of epistemic humility, a bracketing out of at least some of our personal and collective baggage of symbols, historical legacies and "taken-for-granted" assumptions regarding the other (and ourselves as well).

Knowledge *of* others needs to give way to knowledge *for*, and we should be careful to define this *for* in non-ideological terms, without reference to our own fantasies and fears.

Distancing pre-existing commitments (to our own well-being or the well-being of our group, for example) from the concrete shared experiences with the other through which new understandings, re-calibrated power relations and notions of equity may emerge.

Recognize that no one and no people have a monopoly on suffering.

This last "rule" is of great importance. Victimhood is used, time and time again, in contexts great and small, to justify a refusal to engage with the other, to even make the effort to see them; but rather to simplify our interaction and boil it down to a series of demands. Sometimes these demands are material and are accompanied by untold violence as in the examples that follow.

Ethnic conflicts in Ethiopia (between the Tigray, Amhara, and Oromo) are driven by historical grievances, resulting in a war justified by each group's sense of victimhood.

Religious extremism in the Sahel, Nigeria, and Somalia, like Boko Haram's actions, is another instance where groups are using their perceived victimhood to target non-Muslims and even fellow Muslims.

In the Democratic Republic of Congo (DRC), interethnic violence between the Hema and Lendu is sparked by land disputes, fueled by a long history of perceived victimization on both sides.

In Kenya and Uganda, political tribalism often stokes election-related violence, as rival communities like the Kikuyu, Luo, and Luhya justify their actions through a narrative of historical marginalization.

The same can be said of rising hostility toward LGBTQ+ communities in countries like Uganda and Tanzania, where moral and religious victimhood is used to justify state-sponsored discrimination.

The Anglophone-Francophone divide in Cameroon reflects deep resentment, as Anglophones see themselves as victims of decades of marginalization by the Francophone-dominated government, fueling a violent separatist struggle.

We also saw that the Rwanda genocide in 1994 was because of the long-standing tensions between the Hutu and Tutsi in Rwanda which were partly fueled by narratives of victimhood from both sides, each portraying themselves as victims of past oppression and justifying violence in return.

Even, however, on the more micro-level, of schools and universities, sporting events, and school board meetings; issues of gender identity, race and ethnicity are mobilized politically in endless accusations of "transphobic", "toxic masculinity" "racist", "white supremacist". All of which – while in some instances remain tethered to some empirically verifiable event or series of events - actually serve another purpose.

Note that accusing one's adversary of unspeakable crimes leaves the accuser a pure victim as it were. Their suffering then is reason enough not to have to engage in the long, difficult and challenging exercise of engagement with boundaries and communities that any idea of a shared life entails. For this reason, the most important rule of all, the necessary precondition for all else is perhaps the last, namely, *recognizing that no- one and no people have a monopoly on suffering.*

Group Reflection Prompts:

- Think of situations where you came to feel "I have suffered more than..., why is she complaining."
- Think of situations where you came to feel "We have suffered more than his people, why is he complaining?"
- What happens when you let these thoughts lead the conversation?
- What is needed for you to stop these thoughts and see the other's suffering differently?

Between Rights and Community

Today, the most common arguments for how diverse peoples can share a world are predicated on human rights—that is, on law, par excellence. Recent in origin (gaining real traction only in the 1970s), the human rights argument has come to be seen by many as the panacea for almost all social ills, from the evils of social exclusion to different forms of prejudice, oppression, and the refusal to recognize or respect the other. However, this ideology, rooted in universal individualism, overlooks the communal fabric of many societies, certainly African ones, where identity, responsibilities, and moral values are deeply tied to community.

While human rights are important, they are not always aligned with the realities of communal life in Africa and elsewhere. Shorn of any political context, or indeed of any notion of human beings as existing within communities, the ideology of human rights is one of a universal individualism that has led at least one social thinker, Samuel Moyn, to see it as yet another utopic vision destined to fail. Significantly, human rights have never been tied to social rights or social democratic commitments, precisely the "positive liberties" or entitlements that humans can enjoy only within the community.

In many African societies, the notion of rights and the realities of community stand in tension with one another. For instance, African traditional practices, whether related to initiation rites, circumcision, or gender roles, often clash with the universalist lens of human rights. This has been seen in debates over female circumcision (FGM) or the rights of individuals to choose their religion over traditional beliefs. The imposition of international human rights standards on such practices without considering the communal context risks alienating local communities and creating resistance.

A vivid example of this tension can be seen in efforts to promote LGBTQ+ rights in Africa. Western rights-based approaches, emphasizing individual freedoms, have faced strong opposition from communities that see these issues through a collective lens, tied to cultural, religious, and moral codes. For instance, in countries like Uganda, Nigeria, and Kenya, opposition to LGBTQ+ rights is not simply a refusal to recognize individual identities, but rather a defence of what is perceived as communal morality. Imposing abstract human rights standards without addressing the deeper communal context can lead to greater social division rather than integration.

How, then, should we address difference? How should we accommodate particular communities claiming adherence to the authority of a revealed (and hence non-rational) text or of received tradition all containing sets of obligations that are outside the rational discourse of individual and abstract rights? This challenge is compounded by African legal systems, which often retain colonial legal frameworks that emphasize individual rights but fail to recognize the communal dimensions of African life. Traditional forms of justice, such as the *Gacaca* courts in Rwanda or the *Ubuntu* philosophy in Southern Africa, focus on reconciliation, restoration, and communal belonging rather than individual rights alone. These forms of justice emphasize that one's identity is intertwined with the community and that the resolution of conflict must consider the well-being of the group, not just the individual.

Moreover, as seen in conflicts involving pastoralist communities and farmers in West and East Africa, or the displacement of ethnic groups in countries like South Sudan and the Democratic Republic of Congo, human rights frameworks often fail to address the complexities of communal land ownership, resource distribution, and historical grievances. The approach of trying to solve these issues through external legal standards without understanding the local power dynamics and communal relationships can backfire.

This problem, in fact, takes us back to issues of trust and confidence, to membership in and belonging to a moral community, and how the values and defining terms of such a community are markedly different from those of a community based on abstract rights guaranteed by law alone. Yet once we accept the communal aspect of our lives, we are immediately faced with the inherently exclusionary character of such communities and the ensuing challenges posed by that exclusion. How do we ultimately live with difference and share civic space with individuals and groups who embrace a radically different view of the good life, the meaning of divine commands, and the social definitions of communal membership?

The challenge for Africa is not to reject human rights but to integrate them with a deeper understanding of the role of community in social life. Universal rights must be adapted to the diverse contexts of African societies, where moral obligations are often tied to family, tribe, and community. Just as the Rwandan post-genocide reconciliation process took into account local practices of justice and communal healing, the solutions to Africa's crises must come from within the continent's own values and traditions.

We must then explore an alternative to abstract rights, legal formulations, and definitions of human beings as essentially individual agents devoid of collective or communal obligations, commitments, and understandings of self. We need, rather, to review our often less than critical acceptance of the "ideology" of human rights, in any and all circumstances, without attending to the differences of each and every particular case. There are no "best practices" that are applicable globally. There are only the solutions that emerge from within local environments and constraints. Trying child soldiers from northern Uganda at the International Criminal Court may not, at the end of the day, be the most effective way to reestablish social life in a war-ravaged region. Imposing European notions of personhood and gender on the refugee populations of Africa may, similarly, be less than respectful of people's agency and real needs for self-determination.

Rather than imposing foreign norms, Africa needs to find a middle ground—an approach that respects human rights while honouring communal ties. As with the challenges posed by child soldiers in Northern Uganda or the reintegration of displaced populations across the continent, external legal processes such as the International Criminal Court may not always offer the most effective solutions. Instead, African societies must explore local pathways that prioritize communal healing, reconciliation, and the reintegration of those who have been ostracized. We must rather learn to see and respect difference, not simply as producing variants of who "we are," but as constitutive of real, lived differences in individuals and societies—differences that must be factored into our political solutions to social crises.

There is no doubt that such predicated and positionally dependent politics is labour intensive, exhausting and morally challenging. It is also, however, the only serious approach to our current crises in a shared way of life. Ultimately, Africa's way forward lies in embracing its own communal traditions and adapting them to meet contemporary challenges. Addressing difference within African societies requires a blend of respect for human rights and an appreciation of the communal dimensions that define life across the continent. This approach, while complex and challenging, offers the best chance for building a sustainable and inclusive future.

Further Reading

Allport, Gordon. *The Nature of Prejudice.* NY: Doubleday Books, 1954.

Arendt, Hannah. *Responsibility and Judgement. Schocken Books, 2003.*

Dewey, John. *How We Think.* Boston: D.C. Heath & Co., 1910.

Dewey, John. *Democracy and Education.* NY: Dover Books, 2004

Maathai, Wangari. *The Challenge for Africa.* Arrow Books, 2010.

Mamdani, Mahmood. *Citizen and Subject: Contemporary Africa and the Legacy of Late Colonialism.* Princeton: Princeton University Press, 1996.

Oginga Odinga. *Not Yet Uhuru: The Autobiography of Oginga Odinga.* London: Heinemann, 1967.

Seligman, A., Wasserfall, R., Montgomery, D. *Living with Difference: How to Build Community in a Divided World.* Berkeley, University of California Press, 2015.

Wamwere, Koigi wa. *Negative Ethnicity: From Bias to Genocide.* New York: Seven Stories Press, 2003.

Author Profiles

Adam B. Seligman is a Professor of Religion at Boston University. A respected scholar in the fields of civil society and community engagement, he has authored or edited more than two dozen books. He has taught at universities in the United States, Israel, Japan and Hungary, where he was a Fulbright Fellow from 1990 to 1992. His books include: *The Idea of Civil Society* (1992); *Inner-Worldly Individualism* (2016); *The Problem of Trust* (2021); *Modernity's Wager: Authority, the Self and Transcendence* (2000); (with Mark Lichbach) *Market and Community: The Bases of Social Order, Revolution, and Relegitimation* (2000); *Modest Claims: Dialogues and Essays on Tolerance and Tradition* (2004); (with Robert Weller, Michael Puett, and Bennett Simon) *Ritual and its Consequences: An Essay on the Limits of Sincerity* (2008); (with Robert Weller) *Rethinking Pluralism: Ritual, Experience, and Ambiguity* (2012) as well as (with Weller), *How Things Count as the Same: Memory, Mimesis and Metaphor* (2019); and (with Rahel Wasserfall and David Montgomery) *Living with Difference: How to Build Community in a Divided World* (2015).

Prof. Seligman founded the International Summer School on Religion and Public Life in Sarajevo in 2001 and facilitated its growth into CEDAR. He has received the prestigious Dr. Leopold Lucas Prize in 2020 for his work.

Charles Esibikhwa Edward is the Director of the Kenyan Program on Pedagogies for Community (KPPC), with over two decades of experience in community organizing and tribalism engagement in East Africa. He has collaborated with several organizations in his work, including the Institute of Cultural Affairs Kenya (ICAK), the Community Organizing Training Programme (COTP), ICRAF (World Agroforestry-ABCD program), among others, bringing his expertise to the forefront of various impactful initiatives. Beyond his leadership at KPPC, Charles is an Asset-Based Community Development (ABCD) consultant, working with numerous organizations to realize the dream of sustainable development. His consultancy work focuses on empowering communities by leveraging local resources and capacities to foster long-term growth. In recognition of his dedication to community service, he was awarded the 'Spirit of Service' in Community Organization in Kenya in 2019. Additionally, he has been a Fellow of Communities Engaging with Difference and Religion (CEDAR) since 2019, participating in various programmes across East Africa and Asia, further demonstrating his commitment to fostering sustainable, community-centred development.

www.ingramcontent.com/pod-product-compliance
Ingram Content Group UK Ltd.
Pitfield, Milton Keynes, MK11 3LW, UK
UKHW042008190726
13854UKWH00005B/2210

9 789914 760279